"It is quite a feat to write a reflective, historically grounded book about urgency, but James White has accomplished exactly that."

PHILIP YANCEY, *Author of* Reaching for the Invisible God

"James Emery White has done it again. In this new work, *Serious Times*, he has given us not only a thorough analysis of the cultural challenges we currently face but a skillfully developed response that calls for the church to deepen our souls and develop our minds as we seek to answer the call of our day. White's well-written and readable volume is indeed a serious mandate for these serious times. The theological depth and careful thinking displayed throughout the book will strengthen pastors, teachers and laypeople who engage in these important issues. I heartily commend this book."

DAVID S. DOCKERY, *President, Union University*

"My soul is quaking under the impact of this book. Rather than another yawning treatise on cultural demise, Jim White calls us to 'kick at the darkness till it bleeds light.' And the way we kick, he rightly assesses, is with 'deepened souls and developed minds.' Fill our churches, Lord, with such illumined saints, and start with me."

LON ALLISON, *Director, Billy Graham Center, Wheaton College*

BY JAMES EMERY WHITE

Rethinking the Church

A Search for the Spiritual

Life-Defining Moments

A Long Night's Journey into Day

Embracing the Mysterious God

JAMES EMERY WHITE

SERIOUS TIMES

MAKING YOUR LIFE MATTER IN AN URGENT DAY

IVP

InterVarsity Press
Downers Grove, Illinois

InterVarsity Press
P.O. Box 1400, Downers Grove, IL 60515-1426
World Wide Web: www.ivpress.com
E-mail: mail@ivpress.com

InterVarsity Press® is the book-publishing division of InterVarsity Christian Fellowship/USA®, a student movement active on campus at hundreds of universities, colleges and schools of nursing in the United States of America, and a member movement of the International Fellowship of Evangelical Students. For information about local and regional activities, write Public Relations Dept., InterVarsity Christian Fellowship/USA, 6400 Schroeder Rd., P.O. Box 7895, Madison, WI 53707-7895, or visit the IVCF website at <www.intervarsity.org>.

All Scripture quotations, unless otherwise indicated, are taken from the Holy Bible, New International Version®. NIV®. Copyright ©1973, 1978, 1984 by International Bible Society. Used by permission of Zondervan Publishing House. All rights reserved.

Photographs are reprinted with permission. See the illustration credits at the end of the book.

Design: Cindy Kiple

Images: (woman) Rob Krisel/Getty Images
(man) Mel Curtis/Getty Images
(Thomas Jefferson) Getty Images

ISBN-10: 0-8308-3380-3
ISBN-13: 978-0-8308-3380-1

Printed in the United States of America ∞

Library of Congress Cataloging-in-Publication Data

White, James Emery, 1961-
  Serious times: making your life matter in an urgent day / James
Emery White.
    p. cm.
  Includes bibliographical references and index.
  ISBN 0-8308-3380-3 (pbk.: alk. paper)
  1. Christian life. 2. Christian biography. 3. Church history. I.
Title.
BV4501.3.W466 2005
248.4—dc22
                                                                    2005028335

P   18   17   16   15   14   13   12   11   10   9   8   7   6   5   4   3   2

Y   18   17   16   15   14   13   12   11   10   09   08   07

CONTENTS

ACKNOWLEDGMENTS

The vision and influence of several people will be evident to many readers throughout this work; these are most readily acknowledged by the author. Of particular note is Francis A. Schaeffer, who continually attempted to bring together a mind awake to the world, coupled with a life alive to God—all through the lens of an old-fashioned evangelist.

This book was completed while traveling and studying in England, Scotland and France. To the faculty and staff of Oxford University, and the Summer Programme in Theology (through Christ Church College in particular) appreciation is extended for a rich and robust climate of intellectual and spiritual stimulation. I am also grateful to the good folk of Oxford's Eagle and Child pub for providing the perfect setting for many afternoons of writing bliss. Thanks particularly for the parting "Bird and Baby" shirt.

Cindy Bunch, once again my editor at InterVarsity Press, is a gift. I am deeply grateful for her continued support and vision. Thanks also to the team of folks who will make the book known, including Jeff Crosby, Peter Mayer and Brooke Nolen. What a joy the entire IVP team is to work with. For them, books are not simply a business but a mission.

I continue to remain indebted to my assistant, Ms. Glynn Goble, who serves the many aspects of my life and ministry with joy, enthusiasm and continual good humor. Equal thanks to her husband, Bill, for supporting her ministry to my life with ongoing selflessness.

The community of faith known as Mecklenburg Community Church must always be acknowledged—my spiritual home in more ways than one. I often think my role as a pastor is a great cosmic joke, but at least you laugh along with me.

As always, the greatest acknowledgment goes to my family—my wife, Susan, who always makes every page possible, and my four children: Rebecca, Rachel, Jonathan and Zachary, who make every page urgent. My oldest daughter, Rebecca, gave special service by reading the entire manuscript and offering the particularly sage advice of a seventeen-year-old.

My children will undoubtedly live in times more serious than my own. I pray that the spirit of this book will serve them all well.

Ad Majorem Dei Gloriam

INTRODUCTION

"These are the . . . men . . . who understood the times
and knew what Israel should do."

1 CHRONICLES 12:23, 32

My friend," John Adams wrote to Thomas Jefferson toward the end of both of their lives, "you and I have lived in serious times."[1] Indeed they had. The American colony was embroiled in a contentious relationship with its mother country, Britain, which would erupt into a declaration of independence and eventually war. Instead of swift and immediate defeat at the hands of the British, the conflict birthed a new nation that in just over two centuries would be unrivaled in power and influence.

But I will confess to being equally taken by another dynamic: that Adams, Jefferson and the other founding fathers led serious *lives*. Had they not, the course of history would have taken an altogether different turn.

John Adams's life was integrally involved with the Continental Congress, the American Revolution, the writing of Massachusetts' constitution and the negotiation of the Treaty of

Thomas Jefferson

Paris. He served as the first American vice-president under George Washington and then became the nation's second president. Thomas Jefferson drafted the Declaration of Independence and then served as the country's first secretary of state, second vice president

and third president. He fashioned the Louisiana Purchase and
founded the University of Virginia. It is fitting that these founding fathers of America—Adams and Jefferson—died on the same day, July
4, 1826, the fledgling country's fiftieth anniversary.

Serious times met with serious lives. This is the anvil on which
history is forged. More important, it is the means by which the
kingdom of God is advanced and the life of a Christ follower mea-
sured. Paul Helm rightly notes that according to Scripture "the
whole of a person's life is fundamentally serious, something for
which he is responsible before God, and for which he will have to
give an account. . . . He is individually responsible to God for what
he 'makes' of it."[2]

This brings me to a confession. I'm *taken* by this, because there
is nothing I want more than for my life to *matter*. I want to be used
profoundly by God, to be seized by his great and mighty hand and
thrust onto the stage of history in order to do something significant.
With as pure of a heart as I can muster, this isn't about fame or
prestige. It's about wanting my life to count where it is needed
most. There is a great movement of God that has been set loose in
this world, and I want to be on the front lines. And I have felt this
way for a long time.

Between college semesters in the summer of 1980, I went out to
Colorado to work on a project for a company my father was manag-
ing. I took some time off one weekend and went into the city of Fort
Collins. I walked around the campus of Colorado State University,
then made my way to a theater. A new movie had just been released—the second installment of the original Star Wars trilogy, *The
Empire Strikes Back.*

As I am sure you know, the entire Star Wars saga is about the cosmic battle between good and evil, with the first three films focused
on a young farm boy named Luke who becomes swept up in a galactic rebellion against an evil empire.

Seeing that movie long, long ago in a city far, far away at the tender age of eighteen was a defining moment for my life. I walked out of the theater profoundly moved. I remember sitting in my car in the parking lot, overwhelmed with a single thought: *That's what I want for my life: To be caught up in the sweep of history. To be in the center of things. To be making a difference. To be at the heart of the struggle between right and wrong, good and evil.* My heart was almost breaking at the thought of a life of insignificance. I recall thinking, *But where can that happen in the real world? How can I be a part of something that is bigger than I am? Where in life can something so grand be found?*

Then it came to me—as startlingly sudden as a rip of lightning and as poundingly affirmed as any thunder that could follow—*that's what God's invitation to the Christ-life is all about!* There *is* a galactic struggle going on, and I could be a warrior. I could give my life to something that was bigger than I was, that would live on long after I was gone. What I did mattered and could impact all of history—even into eternity. The reality of the spiritual realm, the struggle for men's and women's souls, the cosmic consequences that were at stake—it became so *clear* to me—I could give my life to that! And there was *nothing* that would ever compete with its scale or significance. *Nothing.*

I'm not going to assume you felt the same way following *Star Wars, Braveheart, Lord of the Rings* or any of the scores of other films that have moved me to want to spend my life in great and noble pursuits. But this *is* more than a man's emotional equivalent to chickflicks. *Because you want your life to matter too.*

The moment may not have come seeing William Wallace in full face paint at the battle of Stirling Bridge, or Aragorn wielding the sword of Elendil that had been forged anew. But you *have* been moved, and it was to give your life away to something bigger than you are: to make a difference, to change the world. It may have been seeing *Les Misérables* on stage, reading *The Hiding Place* by Corrie ten Boom, standing on the beach at sunset watching the sun paint its way out of the sky, or sitting on the crest of a mountain at dawn when the blazing newness of the day felt like it was enveloping your very soul. It may have been the stirring of your spirit when you first read a speech by Winston Churchill, or heard an altar call during a Billy Graham crusade, or saw a film showing Mother Teresa ministering in the slums of Calcutta.

Sadly, for most it ends there. The feeling comes and then fades. If it was a film, the closing credits are quickly followed by the trip to the car in the parking lot. If a book, the final chapter lingers only until the phone rings. Even the physical pilgrimage to the historical monument can be quickly eclipsed by an invading horde of school children. But we let it happen!

We allow the movement of God on the surface of our spirits to become lost amid the stones the world tosses thoughtlessly into our lives. As a result, we lose the vision God could give us of our world and our place in it. Too quickly, and often without struggle, we trade making history with making money, substitute building a life with building a career and sacrifice living for God with living for the weekend. We forgo significance for the sake of success and pursue the superficiality of title and degree, house and car, rank and portfolio over a life lived large. We become saved, but not seized; delivered, but not driven.

But it doesn't have to be this way.

During the serious times of Adams and Jefferson, it was unclear whether men and women would rise to the moment. In light of this Thomas Paine authored a series of patriotic tracts called *The Crisis* papers, which appeared in print from 1776-1783. The first of these so stirred George Washington that he ordered it read to his troops late in December 1776 when the American cause seemed to be faltering. "These are the times that try men's souls," Paine's opening sentence began. "The summer soldier and the sunshine patriot will, in this crisis, shrink from the service of his country." He was right. But Paine also understood what would happen if men and women did *not* shrink from a life so spent. So he wrote on: "but he that stands it now deserves the love and thanks of man and woman."[3] Paine's words proved decisive for Washington's troops. Many soldiers whose terms of service would expire that January 1 were inspired to reenlist. Later that same month the Americans won at Trenton, and the tide of the war was turned.

Another revolutionary figure, engaged in a struggle more compelling than the mere birth of a nation, saw the choice men and women make at such moments in history with equal clarity: "You are the light of the world. A city on a hill cannot be hidden. Neither do people light a lamp and put it under a bowl. Instead they put it on its stand, and it gives light to everyone in the house. In the same way, let your light shine" (Mt 5:14-16). Jesus saw the world as a great cosmic contest between good and evil, with the eternity of human souls wavering on the line. He charged those who followed him with the task of engaging the contest in such a way as to make history. We often talk blithely of "seizing the day" as if it was little more than savoring a moment. For Jesus, seizing the day meant responding to the *challenge* of the moment. But where does one begin?

In the ancient Scriptures, a group of men—known as the men of Issachar—were heralded for two things: understanding the times and determining how to live in light of those times (1 Chron 12). This is the combination we must pursue: understanding the serious nature of our time and living intentionally in light of those times. We can deepen our awareness of what is happening in our world—the flow of history to this point and the pivotal moment our day represents—and then explore key areas of our life that need to be developed to live a life of consequence. And doing it *now* matters.

AT THE BEGINNING OF THE SEVENTH AGE

One of the more intriguing observations about the flow of history surfaced in an important essay written just after World War II. Historian Christopher Dawson (1889-1970) suggested that there have been six identifiable "ages" in relation to the Christian church, each lasting for three or four centuries and each following a similar course. Every age begins and ends in crisis. The heart of each crisis is an intense attack by new enemies, inside and outside the church, which in turn demands new spiritual determination and drive.[4] Without this determination and drive, the church would have lost the day. While Dawson accounted for six such ages at the time of his writing, he conceded there may be sixty yet to come before the universal mission of the church is complete.

I contend that we are presently at such an ending and beginning. The crisis is upon us—the enemy is real—and so is the need for those with the spiritual drive and determination to meet the challenge. Yet before we consider our lives, we must consider the times. We must maintain our historical memory of the other ages, particularly the flow of events that led to our current crisis. Apart from this we will be lost in our quest for the Christian response that this day demands, for we will not even recognize the trial.[5]

WORD TO THE READER

You want to enjoy and benefit from your investment of time in reading these pages, and I hope that what I write serves you. So here is what I already know, and you will soon discover.

I have made the first part of this book as accessible as possible. I believe that the call to a serious life is inextricably intertwined with the serious nature of our times, and much of the force of the second half of the book will be lost without the first. However, the history of the "serious times" part of the book may not be to your liking and cause you to lose the motivation to continue on to the "serious lives" section (which is the more familiar terrain of "Christian living"). Simply turn to the interlude and begin there.

Another issue related to the first half of the book is the approach that I take. When writing about history or culture, an author can attempt a broad survey or choose to invest in a narrow study. In other words, you can go a mile wide and an inch deep or an inch wide and a mile deep. There are benefits to both approaches, but drawbacks as well. Broad surveys fall prey to easy critiques of what is *not* said or what is insufficiently nuanced. One will be rightfully tempted to interject, "Yes, the medieval worldview kept God on the throne, but it also kept some pretty vicious kings and popes on thrones; and if you didn't happen to have been born in a privileged class, your life was inevitably nasty, brutish and short." Or "Yes, the Enlightenment may have precipitated a cultural slide into secularism, but it also precipitated things for which I'm thankful, such as universal education, the abolition of slavery, a tripled life expectancy and respect for women and children."

Agreed.

Yet the downside of a focused study is that we can miss the forest for the trees, and such studies are seldom able to engage a popular audience. And if we try for the best of both worlds—sweepingly broad but reasonably exhaustive—we end up with a multivolume work that, again, blocks accessibility to most folks who have a life outside of books. So let me state my boundaries, and perhaps we both can live with the consequences. This book provides a broad overview of history and culture that intentionally has been written for popular appeal. Further, it is also limited to a survey of the West. Finally, it is filled with dead white males, and you should remember that I write as a living one with all of its limiting perspective. Yet I think this still allows the work to tell a very important part of a very large story.

If in the first section the height of our trek through history and culture seems a bit dizzying, the challenge of the second section will be
its weight. Perhaps if we acknowledge this on the front end, and
there is sensitivity to this challenge on both sides, we will be able to
explore much that will stir heart and mind, soul and strength. But it
will be daunting—I know that it has been and continues to be for
me. And yet, serious times demand a serious life.

THE SECOND FALL

"Histories make men wise."

FRANCIS BACON

*"To be ignorant of what happened before you were
born is to remain a child always."*

CICERO

Understanding our day demands understanding the day before.
This means history.

I write these words with a fair amount of hesitation. In high
school many of us were forced to study history under a person singu-
larly gifted to present the subject with numbing dullness. As a result,
many of us read the word *history* and instantly want to close the book
and reach for the remote control—as long as it doesn't turn on the
History Channel.

But history is not simply a cascade of names and dates divorced
from meaning and relevance. *It is the story of our world.* Just as learning about your family of origin helps put the pieces of a larger puzzle
together in terms of who you are, so understanding the flow of events
and ideas from centuries past brings clarity and insight to the present
moment. There is an old adage suggesting that the person who for-
gets history is condemned to repeat it. Perhaps more to the point, the
person who ignores history is condemned to be swept away by its
force. So what do we need to know about the past that has led to the
day we live in?

There has been a second fall.

The first fall led to God's expulsion of humans from the Garden of Eden. The second fall occurred when we returned the favor. The leaders of science and commerce, of education and political machination have ceased operating with any reference to a transcendent truth, much less a deity.

This is a new and profound break with the history of Western thought and culture. Even among those who might be called "pagan," true secularity in this sense has been unknown. Whether the God of Abraham, Isaac and Jacob or the gods of Greece and Rome, generations assumed there was a world beyond the one in which they lived, and they lived accordingly. It would have been alien to their thinking to begin and end with themselves—alone in terms of truth and morality. The second fall changed all of that, and now it shapes the world we live in.

But to feel the *need* to rise to this challenge—much less to actually *rise* to it—demands understanding the grand sweep of ideas and events that have led to this condition. So we must travel back in time, beginning with the Middle Ages, and work our way forward through Western history. There are two ways to take such a journey: one is to go slow, taking many stops along the way; the second is to travel fast and light. We will take the second approach in order to gain a sense of the broad outlines of history—particularly of how far we have fallen and why this moment in time (and our life in it) is so critical.

THE MIDDLE AGES

The foundation of the Western intellectual tradition can be traced back to the Middle Ages. Some may wish to go further, say to classical Greece and Rome, but a growing number of historians, among them Marcia L. Colish in her book *Medieval Foundations of the Western Intellectual Tradition, 400-1400*, have determined that it was during the medieval era that the history of Western culture as we know it began.

The concept of a "Middle Age" can be found as early as Petrarch (d. 1374), a Renaissance scholar who defined historical periods in cultural terms. He perceived that art and language had fallen into decay since the fall of the Roman Empire, which he equated with the sack of Rome in A.D. 410. Petrarch defined the period between 410 and his own day of "rebirth" as an "Age of Darkness," which is why for so long the medieval era was called the Dark Ages.[1] In truth, the medieval era was anything but dark. It witnessed the birth of the university, produced the great writings of Augustine and Aquinas, provided the context for the founding of the influential monastic movement, and gave rise to the engineering marvels of the great cathedrals.

But the brightest light illuminating the Middle Ages was the light of Christ, for the medieval world was profoundly Christian. While the religious beliefs of the common people—often a mixture of pagan thinking and Christian philosophy—were less refined than those of the educated churchmen, their worldview remained thoroughly *spiritual*. And not just *any* spirituality. While many would argue against the Middle Ages as being a "golden age of faith," there is little doubt that a common understanding of the world based on Christian foundations was firmly in place. Reflecting on the popular religious sentiment of the day, historian Christopher Dawson notes that "religion was not a particular way of life but the way of all life."[2] Fellow historian Johan Huizinga contends that the "life of medieval Christendom is permeated in all aspects by religious images. There is nothing and no action that is not put in its relationship to Christ and faith."[3] Men and women living during the medieval era knew they lived in open view of the living God. So while men and women still sinned and fell short of the glory of God, many without shame, they knew they were falling short—and of *what*, and most importantly *Who*. This should not be surprising: "Medieval culture was a culture of the Book," reminds Norman F. Cantor in *The Civilization of the Middle Ages*, "and in the Middle Ages, the Book was the Bible."

God handing St. Peter's keys to the pope and a sword to the emperor

Few mediums provide a clearer window into the soul of an age than art. In our day film presents the clearest view. During the Middle Ages the canvas told the tale. Considering the nature of the time, it should not be surprising that the most depicted scene during the Middle Ages was the crucifixion of Christ. Medieval art was informed by not simply the biblical text but by a profoundly theological understanding of the world and humanity's place in it. Because of the nature of sin in relation to the holiness of God, human beings became inconsequential for artistic representation. Humans remained the object, but not the subject, of art for nearly a millennium.[4]

The reality of a living God so permeated medieval social thinking that there was no doubt of an absolute moral law. Humans did not make laws, they *discovered* them. When a human law conformed to the divine law, it was considered just. When it did not, it was unjust. Little wonder that theology reigned as the queen of the sciences and would remain on this throne throughout the medieval era.

Eventually the deeply entrenched awareness and acceptance of God developed into the full-blown idea of a Christian society. From this, Christendom was born. Following the edict of Emperor Theodosius in 380 mandating that all under his rule profess Christianity, writes historian Martin Marty, "The question was no longer whether society would be Christian, but rather how this was to be realized."[5]

Thus came medieval theocracy, with various twists and turns along the way, but culminating on Christmas Day in 800 when Pope Leo III crowned Charlemagne as emperor and bestowed on him titles that had been reserved for the Roman rulers of the past. This was the strategic union of church and state, religion and society. Though it would quickly descend into a feudal society and become littered with papal and imperial conflict, for the next eight hundred or more years the politics, learning, social organization, art, music, economics and laws of Europe would be "Christian." Not Christian in the sense of fully incorporating the values of the gospel: no one should romanticize the piety of the individual or community during the Middle Ages. In fact, it would be the worldliness of the institutional church toward the end of the Middle Ages that would provide much of the fuel for the Reformation. But the decisively Christian nature of self and society should not be trivialized as merely political either.[6] No matter how much the balance tipped between pope and emperor or church and state, no one could conceive of a secular society. "Even when laymen attacked churchmen," notes J. M. Roberts, "they did so in the name of the standards the Church had itself taught them and with appeals to the knowledge of God's purpose it gave them."[7]

This "medieval synthesis," as it has sometimes been called, brought together the secular and the sacred spheres of life.[8] So despite tensions over power and control, the high point of imperial authority under King Henry I (1002-1024) and King Henry III (1039-1056) was no different in vision from the height of papal authority under Gregory VIII (1073-1085) and Innocent III (1198-1216). The vision for all was a Christian society and to live and act and think Christianly within it.

This was the beginning of our culture. Understanding the West's deeply Christian roots is not meant to envision a return to medieval Christendom or to unduly glorify what was in truth a society with many deficiencies. But it *is* important to establish where our culture began, in relation to things of God and Christianity in particular, in order to grasp how our culture is changing and in which direction Which leads us to the Renaissance.

THE RENAISSANCE

The period known as the Renaissance (fourteenth to sixteenth centuries), which was birthed in Italy but spread gradually to other countries, marked the beginning of the transition from the medieval to the modern world of the seventeenth and eighteenth centuries. As the word itself means, the *Renaissance* was a "*re*-birth" because it was seen as a return to the learning and knowledge reflected in ancient Greece and Rome. It was a turn from the medieval focus on the world-to-come to a fascination with the world-at-hand.

There were many forces that went into the making of the Renaissance, though the most significant development initiating the period was the rediscovery of ancient texts (and ancient languages) and an accompanying set of skills to study them by. The entire rebirth was tied to a recovery of those disciplines, from art to science, which had been lost in the collapse of Roman civilization.[9] So while Leonardo da Vinci wears the famed tag of "Renaissance Man" through his multiple interests and talents, a more accurate example of the rebirth of the classical spirit was Erasmus of Rotterdam (1467-1536). In his studies of the Greek New Testament and the early church fathers, and in his vigorous defense of the pagan classics, Erasmus became a champion of Renaissance discovery. Even the book that made him famous, *Adagia*, reflects the spirit of the day—it was an annotated collection of over three thousand previously unknown Greek and Latin adages.

From the Renaissance came the creation of what many have called "humanism." As the name implies, much of this was simply a celebration of the humanities and humanity itself. Giovanni Boccaccio's *The Decameron*, celebrating life and sensuality, marked a turning point in literature. In art, the medieval hesitance to capture the human image became a distant memory as portraits—both painted and carved—burst onto the scene. Typified by Michelangelo's towering, fourteen-foot sculpture *David*, the human body had been "transfigured into heroic proportions and attitude, not seen since ancient times."[10]

At first this humanism did not involve—much less demand—an undermining of the well-established Christian worldview. In many ways it invigorated it, for the learning was taking place *within* the Christian context that was still in effect from the Middle Ages. As a result, it merely served to expand the existing Christian vision. Social historian Fernand Braudel referred to the early humanism of the Renaissance as a robust and complimentary "dialogue of Rome with Rome," meaning pagan Rome and Christian Rome, between classical and Christian civilization."[11] So during the sixteenth century, Raphael painted the pagan god Apollo on the walls of the papal apartments in Rome. This was not done as a sign of acceptance but of cultural appreciation.[12] This reveals the confidence of the time that knowledge and art were pursued within the context and under the authority of the Christian faith.

So while the early humanism of the Renaissance was built around a return to things classical, it was done in light of the Creator. This was a Christian, or sacred, humanism. Despite some bumps

Michelangelo's *David*

along the road the early humanism of the Renaissance was actually a call for a richer and more well-rounded Christian culture. It was decisively religious and, if anything, was concerned with the renewal rather than the abolition of the Christian church. Thus the cry of *ad fontes*—"back to the sources"—provided devout men and women with the impetus to reach back into the past, beyond any corruption that might have developed in and through the medieval church, to the golden age of the apostolic era. No group would take greater advantage of this than the Reformers. Though disagreement would erupt between the Reformers and the Renaissance humanists, it is often observed that Luther hatched the egg that Erasmus had laid.

Only when humanism was ripped from its Christian moorings and became a *secular* humanism did the interplay between Renaissance humanism and Christianity become adversarial. As Francis Schaeffer puts it in his *Escape from Reason*, when humanism became *autonomous*—meaning divorced from the anchor of biblical revelation and a Christian worldview—it became destructive. Such a return to Athens, independent of Jerusalem, increasingly elevated Plato's contention that "Man is the measure of all things."

This was a radical reversal of medieval understandings, and not unappreciated at the time. William J. Bouwsma, in his study on the waning of the Renaissance, notes the anxiety among many of its leading proponents; many who initially celebrated the humanism of the Renaissance became deeply ambivalent about the future it would bring.[13] With "man," as opposed to God, as the measure of all things, what kind of world would there be? In a bold rejection of previously held truths, values and perspectives, many would claim it to be "enlightened."

THE ENLIGHTENMENT

Those who lived in the eighteenth century had little doubt that they were living in an enlightened age, one that had emerged from a time of twilight. Between 1650 and 1750 lived such luminaries as Sir Isaac Newton, Friedrich Leibniz, John Locke, David Hume, Denis Diderot and Voltaire. Historian Owen Chadwick rightly notes that these were the seminal years of modern intellectual history, and that within this span of time the last remaining vestiges of the Middle Ages ended.[14] But more than an era ended.

"An increasing number of European intellectuals used new ideas about the natural world, society and the nature of things to attack the established churches, to question traditional views of divine revelation," Mark Noll writes, "and even (in an unprecedented step) to doubt the existence of God."[15] Or at least the Christian idea of God as Father. At best, the divine had become a philosophical category, a "first mover" in the grand scheme of things. With the Enlightenment came the "rise of modern paganism."[16]

To properly understand the Enlightenment, it must be seen as more than an age—it was a *spirit* or mood. While the Enlightenment period produced the hymns of Isaac Watts, the deeply Christian music of J. S. Bach, Handel's *Messiah*, German Pietism, the ministries of John Wesley and George Whitefield, and the First Great Awakening, the dominant spirit of the age was anything but Christian. The spirit of the age instead belonged to the *philosophes*, those who embraced the Enlightenment culture and popularized it for all who would listen. And many did.

Henry May captures the spirit of the Enlightenment as the belief in two propositions: first, that the present age is more enlightened than the past, and, second, that we understand nature and humanity best through the use of our natural faculties.[17] The Enlightenment project was the rejection of revelation, tradition or divine illumination as the surest guide for human beings. Instead, autonomous human *reason* reigned supreme. The motto of Immanuel Kant, one of the most significant thinkers of the time, was "Dare to use your own reason" (or simply, "Dare to know").[18]

There are several words worth noting in Kant's challenge: First, the word *dare*, meaning that those who did use reason would inevitably come up against traditional authorities, namely, the church. But that was the point. There could be no authority over the exercise or conclusion of reason. This idea of authority is critical, for the Enlightenment was a rebellion against one source of authority—the church and its appeal to God and his revelation—and the enthronement of another authority, human reason. For someone like the French philosopher Voltaire, the Enlightenment offered emancipation from "prone submission to the heavenly will."

That the reason we use be our *own* also highlights the independence of human intellect, answerable to none and best able to function separate of anything thought to come from God.

Immanuel Kant

And then there is Kant's use of the word *reason*, which for most Enlightenment thinkers, such as the Scottish philosopher David Hume, meant some form of empiricism.[19] Empiricism elevated sense experience above all other sources for gaining knowledge. Sense experience refers to that which can be seen, tasted, touched, heard or smelled. What could not be observed, or at least replicated, was met with skepticism. The fundamental idea was that we could—and should—begin with ourselves and autonomously gain the means by which to judge all things.

The challenge this brought to Christian faith was profound. Alister McGrath charts the development concisely, noting that it was first sympathetically argued that the beliefs of Christianity were rational and thus able to stand up under any amount of intellectual scrutiny. It was then argued that the basic ideas of Christianity, being rational, could be derived from reason *itself*, independent of divine revelation. Then came the final step, the idea that reason was able to stand *over* revelation as judge. If reason was omnicompetent, as Enlightenment thinkers believed, it was supremely qualified to judge Christian beliefs and practices.[20] If reason could not independently produce or verify a particular tenet of Christian faith, then that particular tenet was suspect. Only what human reason could demonstrate became enshrined. While this did not happen overnight, such movements illustrate Henry May's observation that the issue is not about the Enlightenment's relationship *to* religion but rather about the Enlightenment *as* a religion.[21]

The speed by which Enlightenment thinking took hold is breathtaking. Prior to the Enlightenment the unquestioned voice of authority for the Western European mind was that of God himself, particularly as conveyed through the Old Testament writings. Whether the task was reflecting on the history of the human race or the explanation of divine purpose, theology reigned supreme over science and philosophy. It was not that science or philosophy were ignored—only that they were to be submitted to revelation for final interpretation or meaning. Even Descartes, in concluding his *Principes de la philosophie*, wrote "Above all, we will observe as an infallible rule that what God has revealed is incomparably more certain than all the rest." Yet by the end of the seventeenth century the church had been marginalized, theology dethroned as the queen of the sciences and the Christian worldview reduced to a fading memory among the intelligentsia. For the first time since the fourth century, the church would once again face persecution.

What allowed Enlightenment thought to take hold, and with such speed? There can be little doubt that Enlightenment philosophy was reinforced on a popular level by a series of discoveries and breakthroughs that seemed to place reason in charge of public, factual truth and banish biblical revelation to the world of superstition and even outright falsehood. Most well-known is the famed discovery of Copernicus in 1543, verified almost a century later by Galileo, that the earth was not the center of the universe. In determining that we live in a sun-centered universe as opposed to an earth-centered one, the science of Copernicus and Galileo brought into question the trustworthiness of faith itself. At the time, the Catholic Church considered any cosmology other than an earth-centered universe heresy. The Church's position was based on wooden, literal interpretations of narrative texts that described the sun moving and the earth standing still. With the Protestant Reformation ringing in their ears, the Catholic leaders were overly cautious about new interpretations.[22] The turn of events went beyond anyone's imagination. Once Copernicus's theory was proven correct, religious pronouncements on *all* matters of public discourse became suspect.

So while the early writers of the Enlightenment, including René Descartes and John Locke, attempted to put their "enlightened" reflections within a Christian framework, the way had been cleared for others to embark on an increasingly secular assessment of the world. Their growing radical pronouncements fell like seed on fertile soil watered by the headlines of the day. A foundational shift had taken place: from "faith seeking *understanding*" to "faith requiring *justification*."[23] No longer did reason exist to serve faith; faith existed, if at all, on the basis of whether human reason deemed it acceptable.

If the medieval outcome of an entrenched Christian worldview was Christendom, the Enlightenment outcome of the newly entrenched secular humanism was "humandom." The most visible manifestation of this seismic shift was the French Revolution, where a religion of "man" was established. A process of de-Christianization began, so much so that Alexis de Tocqueville would later write that "in France . . . Christianity was attacked with almost frenzied violence."[24] One of the more symbolic events took place on November

10, 1793, when Notre-Dame de Paris, the great church of France—most famous of the Gothic cathedrals—was formally declared and transformed into the Temple of Reason, with busts of Rousseau and Voltaire taking the place of the saints. During the ceremony a hymn to "Liberty" was sung with the following words:

> Descend, O Liberty, daughter of Nature;
> The people have recaptured their immortal power:
> Over the pompous remains of age-old imposture
> Their hands raise thine altar . . .
> Thou, holy Liberty, come dwell in this temple
> Be the goddess of the French.[25]

The second fall was complete.

It has often been observed that ideas have consequences. It's true. They do. When the Christian worldview was jettisoned, the context for belief was severely weakened and eventually removed. God had been silenced and, as a result, made irrelevant. Humans were left to be their own master. Suddenly we lived in a disenchanted world, forced to submit everything to criticism and skepticism.[26]

And it gave us the world we now live in.

A HERO FOR HUMANITY:
THE LIFE OF
WILLIAM WILBERFORCE

William Wilberforce (1759-1833) strode
onto the stage of human history in order
to call the world back to a true view of
humanity in relation to God.

In 1780, after graduating from Cambridge with future prime minister William Pitt the Younger, Wilberforce entered the House of
Commons. While many would look to later events in his life as more
noteworthy, Wilberforce himself pointed to his "great change" during 1784-1785 when he embraced Christianity. "This transformation
redirected the course of his life," writes biographer Kevin Belmonte,
"and without it he would not have become the reformer he was."[1]
Wilberforce himself writes, "The first years that I was in Parliament
I did nothing—nothing I mean to any good purpose. . . . My own distinction was my darling object."[2]

The "great change" changed that.

With his new faith Wilberforce scanned where history had
brought the world, and he saw with new clarity the horrors of one aspect of its arrival—the slave trade. Arguing for a radical reversal of
British policy, Wilberforce stood before Parliament on May 12, 1789,
and for three hours poured out his heart and passion, conviction and
resolve. Speaking to his colleagues of his own pilgrimage on the issue, Wilberforce said:

> I confess to you . . . so enormous, so dreadful, so immediate did
> its wickedness appear, that my own mind was completely made
> up for its abolition. A trade founded in iniquity, and carried on
> as this was, must be abolished, let the policy be what it might—

let the consequences be what they would, I from this time determined that I would not rest till I had [secured] its abolition."[3]

And he did not rest.

For twenty years Wilberforce devoted his life to abolishing Britain's slave trade, and another twenty-six years to abolishing slavery
throughout the British colonies and around the world. Undeterred
by personal challenges to his health and family, death threats and
persecution, world war and prejudice—though it arguably cost him
the role of prime minister of Great Britain—Wilberforce's consistency, courage, disregard for reputation and position, and commitment to Christ allowed him to witness the abolition of Britain's slave
trade throughout the colonies just days before his death.

A life given over to Christ saw the flow of history, and then gave
its life to change it. And did.

THE WORLD THAT LIVES IN US

"Hell is neither so certain nor so hot as it used to be."

BERTRAND RUSSELL

"For thus you speak: 'Real are we entirely,
and without belief or superstition.'
Thus you stick out your chests—but alas—they are hollow!"

FRIEDRICH NIETZSCHE

Sitting in a London pub, I asked the person waiting on me if he could direct me to the home of John Wesley.

"John who?" he replied.

"John *Wesley*," I answered, emphasizing the last name, thinking my American accent might have been confusing.

"Never heard of him," he said. "But hold on, I'll go ask." After approaching three other workers, along with two regulars at the counter, he came back.

"Sorry, can't help. Nobody's heard of him," he said. "Who is he?"

"The founder of Methodism," I replied.

If I had puzzled him before, it had reached new heights.

"Methodism?"

Undaunted, I pressed on. "It's a Christian movement . . . well . . . it *was* a Christian movement within Anglicanism, and then it became a denomination. Wesley was its founder. His home is supposed to be near here."

At the word *Christian* he finally gave a look of recognition. Waving his hand and dismissing the entire conversation with a laugh, he said, "You're at the wrong place to ask about that sort of thing, mate."

Actually, I wasn't.

I was in England, and Wesley is one of England's most historic sons. Educated at Oxford, Wesley was a member of the Church of England his entire life, though his successors would take his methodical approach to Christianity and begin ordaining ministers under the name "Methodist" shortly after his death. His portrait hangs prominently in Oxford's Christ Church College dining hall to this day. But it wasn't just Wesley's English roots that had me in the right place or that I was asking about him in London, just blocks away from his home. Here was one of religious history's most towering figures and founder of one of the world's largest Christian denominations—completely unknown to everyone who had been asked.

Welcome to our world.

If history retraces our steps to the present, then the social sciences invite us to understand where we now find ourselves. Sociologist Peter Berger, among many others, has suggested that the modern world is now being shaped by three fast-moving cultural currents: secularization, pluralization and privatization.[1] Big words. Even bigger ideas.

THE PROCESS OF SECULARIZATION

The English word *secular* derives from the Latin *saeculum*, which means "this present age." The contemporary term *secular* is descriptive of that which is divorced from religious or spiritual sensibility—and looking back to the ancient Latin usage, it enthrones that which is of this world. *Secularization* is the process by which something *becomes* secular. And it is this cultural current which is raging through our world like a flash flood.

As a result, the church has largely lost its influence as a shaper of life and thought in the wider social order, and Christianity has lost its place as the dominant worldview. Richard John Neuhaus writes that we live in a "naked public square," meaning that religious ideas and mores no longer inform public discourse.[2] Christianity has ceased to be the motivating center of Western life; the religious question is consciously or unconsciously pushed from the heart of human concerns; and the institutional forms of Christianity have, and are, undergoing revision at the hands of the "world."[3]

In his *Guide for the Perplexed*, author E. F. Schumacher relates his experience of getting lost during a sightseeing trip to Moscow during the Stalinist era. With map in hand, Schumacher engaged a government tour guide, who showed him where he was in relation to the map.

"But these large churches around us," Schumacher objected to the guide, "they're not on the map."

The guide replied tersely, "We don't show churches on our maps."

"But that can't be," Schumacher insisted. "The church on *that* corner is on the map."

"Oh, that," the guide replied. "That *used* to be a church. Now it's a museum." That, Schumacher went on to conclude, was the point. Those things that humankind has most believed in are no longer on the map of reality, or if they are, they are relegated to a museum. In reflecting on Schumacher's story, Huston Smith notes that our world "has erased transcendence from our reality map."[4]

Yet a full-blown secularization "thesis" has been challenged.[5] There's no debate about the reality of the process itself; what is debated is the degree to which the process of secularization can redirect a person from a belief in God. This is particularly an American debate, for while the process of secularization is clear, it has yet to produce an overwhelmingly secularized population. Our day is, as Peter Berger himself observes, "as furiously religious as it ever was, and in some places more so than ever."[6] German philosopher Friedrich Nietzsche may have proclaimed God dead, but it is apparent that few in America attended the wake.

It may be premature, though, to declare secularization culturally real but privately irrelevant. Consider the already deeply entrenched secularity—public and private—of Western Europe. Perhaps even more striking is the secularized nature of the American educational system, the mass media and the upper echelons of the legal system. These are the epicenters of culture—the means by which values and ideas come into being and are disseminated. While their forces may be "relatively thin on the ground," Berger observes, "they are very influential, as they control the institutions that provide the 'official' definitions of reality."[7] Berger quips, "If India is the most religious country on our planet, and Sweden is the least religious, America is a land of Indians ruled by Swedes."[8] So a country like the United States is clearly secularized politically and, arguably, intellectually; it just may take a while for it to get to the average person. But it may come sooner than we think.

Think about how faith itself is tended—it needs *support*. Apart from nurture by a Christian community, faith quickly withers. We need a context of encouragement. Beliefs don't exist in a vacuum. They need to be nurtured, reinforced. A secularized world no longer offers the deep religious socialization and the frequent reaffirmation of beliefs necessary for a distinctive faith to flourish. The declining social significance of religion will inevitably cause a decline in the *number* of religious people and the *extent* to which those people are religious. When society no longer supports religious affirmation, the difficulty of maintaining a solitary faith increases dramatically.

A 2003 survey found that overall belief in God among Americans had dropped to 79 percent, with only 66 percent feeling certain about it. Astonishingly, 10 percent of those who call themselves Protestants, 21 percent of confessing Roman Catholics and 52 percent who profess to be Jews don't believe in God.[9] Another 2003 survey revealed that now 60 percent of all Americans believe that cohabitation is morally acceptable, with 42 percent approving a sexual relationship with someone of the opposite sex other than their spouse. These were significant increases compared to surveys conducted even two years earlier. The approval of gay sex alone increased by 20 percent during the twenty-four-month span.[10] It is difficult to deny secularization: religious observance is in decay, key beliefs are being abandoned, previously expected marks of behavior are being dropped and the boundary lines between people of faith and the rest of the world are being eroded. Coupled with the declining effectiveness and even the will of the church to stem the tide, the process of secularization will continue to course through culture, cutting deep channels into institutions *and* persons.

This is what historian Owen Chadwick was referring to when he noted that "Enlightenment was of the few. Secularization is of the many."[11] The *very* many.

THE PROCESS OF PRIVATIZATION

Ray Kroc, the man who turned McDonald's into a fast-food franchise, was once quoted as saying, "I believe in God, family, and McDonald's. And in the office, that order is reversed."[12] Not many in our world would find fault with his approach.

Privatization is the process by which a chasm is created between the public and the private spheres of life, and spiritual things are increasingly placed within the private arena.[13] So when it comes to things like business, politics or even marriage and the home, personal faith is bracketed off. The process of privatization, when left unchecked, makes the Christian faith a matter of personal preference, trivialized to the realm of taste or opinion.[14] This trend was evident to historian Theodore Roszak, who remarked that Christian faith in America is "socially irrelevant, even if privately engaging."[15]

The influence of privatization is profound. Faith does not simply have a new home in our private lives; it is no longer accepted outside of that sphere. More than showing poor form, talk of faith has been banished from the wider public agenda. As historian and educator Page Smith sarcastically observed, in our day "God is not a proper topic for conversation, but 'lesbian politics' is."[16] But privatization goes farther. Once placed solely within our private worlds, faith becomes little more than a reflection of ourselves.

Sociologist Robert Bellah interviewed a young nurse named Sheila, who captured this spirit well: "I believe in God. I'm not a religious fanatic. I can't remember the last time I went to church. My faith has carried me a long way. It's Sheilaism. Just my own little voice."[17] Spirituality has become anything an individual desires it to be, a private affair to be developed as one sees fit. The process of privatization has created a context where spirituality has finally met secular humanism, for spirituality has become not only privatized but autonomous.[18]

THE PROCESS OF PLURALIZATION

I'm a fan of the old Andy Griffith TV series. Near my home in Charlotte is Mt. Airy, North Carolina, the real hometown of Andy Griffith and the inspiration for Mayberry. The small hamlet annually holds a Mayberry Day festival that attracts thousands. One year my family and I attended the festival, and we could readily see how the little town had shaped the series. The quaint downtown, the diner—there was even Floyd's Barber Shop.

If you've ever watched the series, still in heavy syndication, you know that when Andy's deputy, Barney Fife, asks his long-time girlfriend, Thelma Lou, out for a date, more often than not he asks, "Want to go to the picture?" He means the film at the movie theater. Which movie would they see? *The* movie. There was only one. It would change from time to time, causing an excited stir in the little town and an occasion for another outing, but there would only be *one* film showing.

Today, Barney and Thelma Lou would have a time of it. We go to a cineplex and choose from twenty or more films, each one assaulting our senses through marketing and promotion. The simple "Want to go to the picture?" isn't so simple anymore. It's not even the right question. That is the heart of pluralization.

The process of pluralization occurs when individuals are confronted with a staggering number of ideologies and faith options competing for their attention.[19] Peter Berger speaks of the traditional role of religion as a "sacred canopy" covering the contemporary culture. Religion, at least in terms of the idea of there being a God that life and thought had to consider, blanketed all of society and culture. Today that canopy is gone, replaced instead by millions of small tents under which we can choose to dwell.[20]

There can be little doubt that the fuel that powered this process, at least in the United States, was immigration. One visit to Ellis Island will drive this home: inside the main visitors' center is a visual display of the tidal wave of immigration that struck upon the shores of our country. Between 1901 and 1910, nearly nine million immigrants were admitted to America, the majority from Southern and Eastern Europe. Nearly six million more would come during the following decade. By 1910 alone, 40 percent of the population of New York City was foreign-born.[21] And they brought their religions with them.

But pluralization means far more than a simple increase in the number of faith options. The sheer number of choices and competing ideologies suggest that no one perspective or religious persuasion has the inside track on the spiritual realm.[22] Theologian Langdon Gilkey is correct when he observes that "many religions have always existed"; what is unique is a "new consciousness" that "entails a feeling of rough parity . . . among religion." By *parity*, Gilkey means "the presence of both truth and grace in other ways."[23]

Ellis Island (1904)

Malise Ruthven calls America the "divine supermarket." The technical term for this is *syncretism*, the "mix and match" mentality of pulling together different threads in various religions in order to create a personal religion that suits individual taste. Christianity becomes one of many competing boutique worldviews, no better or worse than another, which has set up shop in society's mall for people to sample as a matter of personal preference. Instead of resisting this devaluation of truth, many within the world's religious bodies have decided to embrace the idea. As a Jewish rabbi and a Catholic Monsignor put forward in a joint writing, searching for God has become like climbing a mountain. Since everyone *knows* that there is not just *one* way to climb a mountain—mountains are simply too big for that—there are any number of paths that can be taken. So, the rabbi and priest conclude, all of the ideas about God throughout the religions of the world are like different ways up the mountain, and all of the names of God in all of the world's religions all name the same God. The Dalai Lama, who wrote the foreword to the book, heartily agreed.[24]

So while Christianity used to be rejected by Enlightenment intellectuals because its central beliefs supposedly had been disproven by science or philosophy, today orthodox Christianity tends to be disqualified on the grounds that it argues for an unchanging and universal truth.[25] A particular faith used to be discredited on the basis of what was perceived to be truth; now a faith is wrong for claiming there *is* truth.

THE WORLD THAT LIVES IN US

Recently, a category two hurricane made landfall on the coast of North Carolina. Hurricane Isabel's torrential rain, one-hundred-mile-per-hour winds and pounding seas lashed the Outer Banks.

Utne Reader, July-August 1998, "Designer God"

Once the skies cleared, more than wreckage and downed power lines were left behind. The geography of the coast itself had been changed. Fifteen- to twenty-foot sand dunes were gone. Highway 12 ended in the ocean; pelicans were flying over water where the road once ran. The new inlet was actually deep enough for small boats to pass through. The hurricane so altered the existing terrain that new islands were formed.[26]

In similar fashion the currents coursing through our culture are leaving their marks on society's landscape. Four marks, to be exact: moral relativism, autonomous individualism, narcissistic hedonism and reductive naturalism.[27] Again, big words. But even bigger realities.

MORAL RELATIVISM

Recently, when logging-on to the opening page of America Online, the feature "tease" was "Live Together and Save Money," suggesting that I should "go the domestic partner route." One click away was a collection of articles headlined with "Living in Sin and Loving the Savings." The short, descriptive paragraph proclaimed: "More and more couples are shacking up rather than getting hitched. And why not? These days, live-ins are eligible for many new financial perks."[28]

The guiding motif of the modern world is found in the phrase "And why not?"

This is moral relativism. Basically it says, What is true for you is true for you, and what is true for me is true for me. What is moral is dictated by a particular situation in light of a particular culture or social location. Few books championed this value more directly than Joseph Fletcher's *Situation Ethics*. Fletcher challenged the role of rules in making moral decisions, maintaining that a person must determine in each situation what is the most appropriate thing to do. If it is determined that what is appropriate demands the suspension of established rules, so be it. Moral values become a matter of personal opinion or private judgment rather than something grounded in objective truth. This is now so entrenched that Allan Bloom, reflecting on his role as a university educator, maintains that there "is one thing a professor can be absolutely certain of. Almost every student entering the university believes, or says he believes, that truth is relative."[29]

The radical nature of this new but defining characteristic should not be missed. It is not simply that people are less moral today than in previous years (though they arguably are): recent studies now indicate that lying is a part of our culture—a trait of American character—and that one-third of all married men and women have had at least one affair.[30] Whether we would have found these same moral conditions a generation ago is not the point. What *has* emerged in new and startling ways is the claim that things such as lying and adultery are no longer *wrong*. To borrow from the prophet Jeremiah, we have become a people who do not even know how to blush (Jer 6:15). We no longer even think we *need* to. Today, "a man may be greedy and selfish; spiteful, cruel, jealous, and unjust; violent and brutal; grasping, unscrupulous, and a liar; stubborn and arrogant; stupid, morose, and dead to every noble instinct," to borrow from Dorothy L. Sayers, "and still we are ready to say of him that he is not an immoral man."[31] And we certainly are not going to say it of ourselves.

AUTONOMOUS INDIVIDUALISM

"Man is the being whose project is to be God."[32] This penetrating assessment, offered from the French existentialist philosopher Jean Paul Sartre, is particularly accurate of modern humans.

In reviewing the past five hundred years of Western cultural life, Jacques Barzun concluded that one of the great themes is "emancipation," the desire for independence from all authority. Barzun concludes that for the modern era it is perhaps the most characteristic cultural theme of all.[33] "Autonomous individualism" maintains that each person is independent in terms of destiny and accountability.

Ultimate moral authority is *self*-generated. In the end we answer to no one but ourselves because we are truly on our own. Our choices are ours alone, determined by our personal pleasure, and not by any higher moral authority. Intriguingly, Thomas Oden notes that this is the force behind the idea of heresy. The "key to 'hairesis' (root word for 'heresy') is the notion of choice—choosing for *oneself*, over against the apostolic tradition."[34]

The individualism of the modern world first took root during the Reformation. The Reformation made the pursuit and practice of faith a matter of personal responsibility. The will of God was to be determined individually and then followed. But by the second half of the nineteenth century, this individualism morphed into the idea of having the right to do whatever you wanted provided it did not harm others. After World War II the idea of individualism shifted yet again, even to the point of changing the scope of the question: "We claim not only the right to do what is right in our own eyes but to assert that the world is as we variously see it."[35]

This same spirit of autonomous individualism erected the infamous tower of Babel and is leading to its rebuilding today. Only this time we are not building with bricks and mortar but with silicon chips and genetic engineering. We live in a technological age and have embraced technological advance with abandon, creating what Neil Postman termed a "technopoly," where technology of every kind is cheerfully granted sovereignty.[36]

Ironically, within the word *technology* itself lies the new philosophical mooring that marks our intent. The word is built from such Greek words as *technitēs* (craftsman) and *technē* (art, skill, trade), which speak to the idea of either the person who shapes or molds something or to the task of shaping and molding. But it is the Greek word *logos*, to which *technitēs* is joined, that makes our term *technology* so provocative. Within Greek thought *logos* is a reference to divine reason, or the organizing principle of the world. In

John's Gospel *logos* is used to communicate the idea of the divinity of Jesus. Moderns have put together two words that the ancients would not have dared to combine, for the joining of the words intimates that mere humans can shape the very order of the world. Though technology itself may be neutral in its enterprise, there can be no doubt that within the word itself are the seeds for the presumption that would seek to cast God from his throne and assert humanity in his place as the conduit of divine power.[37] And we have wasted little time.

On July 25, 2003, the first test-tube baby turned twenty-five. Robert Edwards, who along with his partner Patrick Steptoe pioneered the procedure, graced the occasion with a rare but candid interview with *The Times* of London. "It was a fantastic achievement but it was about more than infertility," said Edwards, then seventy-seven and emeritus professor of human reproduction at Cambridge University. "I wanted to find out exactly who was in charge, whether it was God Himself or whether it was scientists in the laboratory."

Smiling triumphantly at the reporter, he said, "It was us."[38]

NARCISSISTIC HEDONISM

In Greek mythology Narcissus is the character who, on seeing his reflection in the water, becomes so enamored with himself that he devotes the rest of his life gazing at his own reflection. From this we get our term *narcissism*, the preoccupation with self.

Narcissistic hedonism is the classic "I, me, mine" mentality that places personal pleasure and fulfillment at the forefront of concerns. Or as Francis Schaeffer maintained throughout his writings, the ultimate ethic of our day is the pursuit of personal peace and individual affluence. Noted cultural historian Christopher Lasch christened ours "the culture of narcissism," positing that the current taste is for individual therapy instead of religion. The quest for personal well-being, health and psychic security has replaced the older hunger for personal salvation.[39] It is as if we have settled for a redemption that salvages this world alone. Therapeutic culture makes well-being *everything*. There is no longing for heaven to lift our gaze beyond the pale of this world and no fear of hell to drive us to forsake it.

This runs deeper than mere self-gratification. Narcissism has become a guiding worldview. Stanley Grenz observes that Anselm's famed dictum "I believe in order that I may understand" was altered by the Enlightenment to become "I believe what I can understand."[40] The modern twist goes further, becoming "I believe when I understand that it helps me."

Such pragmatism has been seen before. Many have wondered how Hitler could have advanced his horrific agenda through the German Republic, culminating in World War II and the holocaust. While complex and multifaceted, a key was the promised utopia of personal peace and affluence. This then became the basis of what was accepted as moral and true. Historian Michael Burleigh's assessment is that there was simply a moral collapse as people "chose to abdicate their individual critical faculties in favor of politics based on faith, hope, hatred and sentimental collective self-regard for their own race and nation."[41]

In the end the Germans found that such preoccupation with self failed to deliver. As Daumier depicted Narcissus in a series of lithographs on the ancient Greek and Roman myths, the reflection that so captivated his life was not in fact an accurate portrait. H. R. Rookmaaker notes that, thin and gaunt, almost comical in face, Narcissus was a "starving idiot, grinning at his own hollow cheeks."[42] Feasting on yourself is a very sparse meal.

REDUCTIVE NATURALISM

Gerard Piel, founder and publisher of *Scientific American* magazine, has argued that when historians examine Western civilization of the twentieth century, it will be deemed the "age of science." Not only have the practical details of daily life been transformed by scientific advances, but the sense of who we are, how our world came to be, our role in it, our origins and even ultimate fate have been influenced by scientific thinking as never before.[43]

But in terms of the world living in us, this elevation of science has taken a particular turn. Scientist Ian Barbour offers a firsthand analysis, noting that when religion first met modern science in the seventeenth century, the encounter was a friendly one. "By the eighteenth century many scientists believe in a God who had designed the universe, but they no longer believe in a personal God actively involved in the world and human life. By the nineteenth century," Barbour concludes, "scientists were hostile to religion."[44] And the crux of that hostility is rooted in what can be called a "reductive naturalism."

Naturalism entails the idea that nature is "all that is." "Reductive" naturalism holds that only those things that can be empirically verified in nature can be known. So a reductive naturalism contends that what is real is only that which can be seen, tasted, heard, smelled or touched and then *verified*, meaning it can be scientifically replicated. Knowledge is "reduced" to this level of knowing. If it cannot be examined in a tangible, scientific manner, it is not simply unknowable, it is meaningless.

This naturalism holds that life is accidental. There is nothing beyond ourselves that will ever bring order, reason or ultimate explanation to our lives. We must restrict what can be known to what is immediately before us, to what is "given" or "factual"—what can be empirically, or scientifically, demonstrated. As astronomer Carl Sagan argued in his final work, the goal is to rid ourselves of a "demon-haunted" world, meaning anything that would challenge the rule of science and technology as the ultimate arbiter of truth and reality, for there is no other truth or reality to embrace.[45] So much for God.

Of course science has never been the antagonist that many have made it out to be, nor does Christianity deserve the reputation developed during the eighteenth and nineteenth centuries as the primary obstacle to scientific progress.[46] The critical issue is the philosophical interpretations that some scientist have attached to their discoveries. As Colin Brown has noted, scientific interpretations often have "their roots in . . . ancient pagan philosophy."[47] Scientists tend to be poor philosophers and even worse theologians. Yet modern cosmologists eagerly speak to issues of faith and philosophy, often with greater authority—and audiences—than priests and theologians.[48] So we do not simply have science but *scientism*—the deification of scientific methods and results as religion. No longer is it simply a question of whether a test-tube can prove God; the test-tube *is* God.

Scientist Louis Pasteur as "Le Bon Pasteur" ("the good shepherd").
Cartoon by Alfred Le Petit.

MODERNITY'S WAKE

For Christians, understanding the world we live in is decisive on two fronts. First, we must be on guard in relation to how this world might be living in *us*. Do we think Christianly, or have we bought into a kind of reductive naturalism? Are our souls informed and directed by the authority of Scripture and the leading of the Holy Spirit, or have we succumbed to the subtle temptation of moral relativism? Do we mark our years by dedication to God and his eternal purposes, or do we strip our lives of any sense of calling and answer only to the voice of an autonomous individualism? Do we live in light of the great redemptive drama, selflessly giving ourselves to the advance of the kingdom and the building of the church, or do we find ourselves drifting into a narcissistic hedonism that makes all spiritual alignments a consumer affair?

Second, we also need to understand the world in order to discern its presence in the lives of those around us. What has the world done to them? How might we begin to live, speak and serve in ways that intersect with the deep needs the world has left unmet? And it has left much unmet.

The trauma of our world is that the processes of modernity have failed to deliver. Rather than enhancing personal satisfaction and fulfillment, we live in a barren wasteland. *Moral relativism* has led to a crisis in values; we find ourselves needing values but not having them, and we are divorced from any means of finding them. *Autonomous individualism* has led to a lack of vision; there is nothing calling us upward to be more than we naturally are. *Narcissistic hedonism* has fostered empty souls; anyone who has followed its ever-deadening trail knows how hollow its entreaties are. *Reductive naturalism* has proven inadequate for human experience; we intuitively know that there is more to reality than what we sense empirically.

The inability for life to fully function apart from God was seen by many from the beginning. Voltaire himself refused to let men talk atheism in front of the maids. "I want my lawyer, tailor, valets, even my wife, to believe in God; I think that if they do I shall be robbed less and cheated less."[49]

Such sentiments led the historian Christopher Dawson to the central thesis of his life's work: not simply that you cannot study culture apart from religion but that culture cannot *survive* without religion.[50] This is the world's great quandary. We are not plagued by the first part of Nietzsche's famous claim—that God is dead—but increasingly by his less well-known assertion that "we have killed him." From this comes the true challenge of the modern world: "How shall we, the murderer of all murderers, comfort ourselves?"[51]

STANDING IN THE STORM:
THE LIFE OF
DIETRICH BONHOEFFER

Faced with a mounting assault on the citadels of faith in a modern world, in a culture
increasingly devoid of values, one man
stood on principle and challenged the direc-
tion of an entire nation that had hurled itself headlong into the abyss
of depravity.

Dietrich Bonhoeffer (1906-1945) was a German pastor who lived
under the dark shadow of the swastika in Nazi Germany. Speaking
out against Hitler's atrocities from the beginning, Bonhoeffer was ar-
rested for his role in the resistance movement and was executed on
April 9, 1945, by special order of Heinrich Himmler. Such a sacrifice
was not only accepted by Bonhoeffer but anticipated; six years prior
to his imprisonment he wrote "When Christ calls a man, He bids
him come and die."[1]

In the face of a modern world gone mad, Bonhoeffer went deep
in his musings on what it meant to be a Christian in a secular world.
From the beginning of the Nazi ascension to power in 1933,
Bonhoeffer launched himself into the fray of protest, particularly
against the insidious rise of anti-Semitism. He soon became a leading voice for the Confessing Church, which led the way for German
Protestant resistance to Hitler and the Nazi regime. For Bonhoeffer
the resistance was not political but spiritual; it was a matter of discipleship. His allegiance was to "a Lord who outweighed the Fuhrer,"
knowing that "only such a lordship and such a radical discipleship
could trump the claims and manipulation of the German state."[2]

In 1935 Bonhoeffer organized and then led a new seminary at
Finkenwalde, where he established a communal life that stood in

stark opposition to the forces at work around him. Shut down in
1937, it continued in secrecy as an underground fellowship until
1940. As described in his book *Life Together*, Bonhoeffer determined
to live—and draw others to live—the Christian life in the face of a
secular world. But rather than withdraw from the world, this became
the basis for his engagement of the world. Writing to fellow theologian Reinhold Niebuhr about those who encouraged him to leave
Germany, Bonhoeffer was adamant: "I will have no right to participate in the reconstruction of Christian life in Germany after the war
if I do not share the trials of this time with my people."[3]

His last weeks were spent in various Gestapo prisons with men and
women of many nationalities, finally ending in Flossenburg. One of
his fellow prisoners, an English officer, wrote that Bonhoeffer

> was one of the very few persons I have ever met for whom God
> was real and always near. . . . On Sunday, April 8, 1945, Pastor
> Bonhoeffer conducted a little service of worship and spoke to us
> in a way that went to the heart of all of us. He found just the right
> words to express the spirit of our imprisonment, the thoughts
> and the resolutions it had brought us. He had hardly ended his
> last prayer when the door opened and two civilians entered.
> They said, "Prisoner Bonhoeffer, come with us." That had one
> meaning for all prisoners—the gallows. We said good-by to him.
> He took me aside: "This is the end, but for me it is the beginning
> of life." The next day he was hanged in Flossenburg.[4]

In the face of a modern, secularized world, Dietrich Bonhoeffer
demonstrated more than the cost of discipleship; he demonstrated
its call.

THE CITY OF
DREADFUL DELIGHT

"O tempora, o mores" ["O, what times. O, what behavior!"]

CICERO

"I don't think we're in Kansas anymore."

DOROTHY, *THE WIZARD OF OZ*

In her book on nineteenth-century London, *The City of Dreadful Delight,* Judith Walkowitz describes the Victorian town as both a site of liberation and genuine danger. Women were given opportunities unheard of in previous centuries. They could get jobs, buy homes and walk down the street on their own. But such freedom came at a price.[1]

Exploitation, constant fear of the loss of employment and homelessness also came into view. Though liberated from the control of families, they were now unprotected and subject to assault. The city was full of delights; it was also made dreadful by danger.

We now live in an *age* of dreadful delight. The modern world—a world with virtually unlimited scientific and technological promise, free of moralistic inhibitions that would seem to hamper the pursuit of personal fulfillment—is also full of dread. And some are just now beginning to feel it.

Those who do, call their feelings "postmodern."

The prefix *post* means "after," so the term *postmodern* refers to the time after the modern era. Whether or not we are actually in such a time, more than chronology was at hand when the term was introduced in Jean-François Lyotard's *The Postmodern Condition.* There was a keen and intuitive sense that something new was beginning to take hold of our culture.

To understand this, theologian Stanley Grenz suggests reflecting on the difference between the original *Star Trek* and its contemporary offshoots, such as *Star Trek: The Next Generation.* The logical, emotionally disdaining Spock—the epitome of the Enlightenment man—is replaced by the android Data, who wishes for nothing *more* than emotions as he realizes that his all-consuming rationality leaves him incomplete and less than human. The captain's chair, once filled by the alpha-male James T. Kirk, is now occupied by the thoughtful Jean-Luc Picard, who seeks the empathetic insights of a female counselor long before charging up the phaser banks. But the changes run deeper than the makeup of the characters. In the new world of *The Next Generation* "time is no longer simply linear, appearance is not necessarily reality, and the rational is not always to be trusted."[2]

Most would agree that whatever is happening, it is not so much the demise of modernity as the *exhaustion* of modernity.[3] As Jacques Barzun has concluded, we now live in a time of "decadence." For Barzun this is not a moral statement but one that harkens back to the literal sense of the word—that of a "falling

Cast of original *Star Trek*

off." This is a restless time because there are few lines of clear advance. Forms of art, as of life, seem tired. Boredom and fatigue have set in. This has bred hostility to things as they are, thus the birth of the dismissive prefix *post*, as if dismissing the past will usher in a new day.[4]

Or as one of the musical voices of postmoderns, Avril Lavigne, sings:

It's a d*** cold night
Trying to figure out this life
Won't you take me by the hand
take me somewhere new
I don't know who you are
But I'm, I'm with you.

David Harvey's conclusion that postmodernism is a kind of crisis within modernism seems apt. Or as Neil Smith quipped, "The Enlightenment is dead, Marxism is dead, the working class movement is dead . . . and the author does not feel very well either."[5] There can be little doubt that modernity created the world in which we live and much of the world that lives in us; the currents of postmodernism mirror the morning-after hangover—we are trying to sort out the night before so that we can get a handle on the day at hand.

So we need to understand the beginning movements of postmodern*ism*.[6] Postmodernism marks the intellectual mood and the wide array of cultural expressions that seem to be challenging many of the existing forms and dynamics created by modernity. Postmodern*ity* is the *era* in which we live; postmodern*ism* is an *outlook* taking root and increasingly shaping our ideas, attitudes and values.

A CHANGING VIEW OF REALITY

Plato suggested that we imagine a man in a cave bound in chains, unable to turn around and see what is behind. Thus confined, he is forced to look at the back wall of the cave, where he sees the dancing shadows of light coming from a fire at the mouth of the cave. This is all of reality to the man in the cave. He sees nothing but the dancing shadows because he is unable to turn to see what is behind him. Plato used this image to challenge the limits of human knowledge. In our day, it is a metaphor for the growing conviction that all we "know" is vague, separate from ultimate truth; we are unable to see the world as it is.

The Enlightenment was based on a set of foundational assumptions about reality, specifically how knowledge *relates* to reality. Knowledge was assumed to be certain, objective, good and accessible to the human mind. There was confidence in the capacities of human reason to not only discover knowledge but for that knowledge to be unbiased and universal. Through reason a person could determine what "is" finally and definitively. The postmodern spirit is beginning to turn its back on the "foundationalism" of modernity—the idea that what can be known is built on an indubitable foundation of observable facts. Even the *quest* for objective, universal knowledge is increasingly rejected. Gary Woller writes that "postmodernism is about deposing the trinity of the Enlightenment—reason, nature and progress—which presumably triumphed over the earlier Trinity."[7]

Much of this is based on the growing sense that no one is truly objective. We cannot stand outside of our own context—including experiences, biases and historical-cultural current—and be free to make an unconditioned observation. More than the sentiment "That's your opinion," the idea is that *everything* is opinion. This does not mean that there's not a reality "out there," just that all of our "stories" about what is "out there" are the products of individual, highly subjective minds engaging "what is." The words and ideas we end up having to use may be quite limited and unique to ourselves.

The philosopher Ludwig Wittgenstein illustrated this concern with the following picture. Take a look at it, and ask yourself what it is.

Do you see a duck or a rabbit? Approached from the left we see the bill of a duck. Approached from the right, we see a rabbit with outstretched ears. The picture didn't change—it is what it is—but it can be interpreted in either fashion with integrity. This is at the heart of the new confusion over "reality." While not open to endless interpretations—it may be a rabbit or a duck, but it certainly is not the engineering plans for a space shuttle—it represents the way many postmoderns tend to think about the world: that reality is little more than what individuals perceive it to be.

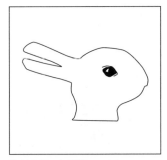

Rabbit/Duck, Wittgenstein

Walter Truett Anderson illustrates this shift in how we view the world with a story of three umpires having a beer after a baseball game. One says, "There's balls and there's strikes, and I call 'em the way they are." A second replies, "There's balls and there's strikes, and I call 'em the way I see 'em." The third says, "There's balls and there's strikes, and they ain't *nothin'* until I call 'em."[8]

Much of this was first espoused by someone who died long before the postmodern era began. Friedrich Nietzsche (1844-1900) was a postmodern before postmodern was cool, devoting his life to exposing Enlightenment optimism, never dreaming it would be a century later that his thought would begin to take popular root.[9] Though Nietzsche's ideas ranged far wider than what is reflected in the current postmodern mood, his conviction that there are no facts, only interpretation, has begun to take hold. Nietzsche contended that knowledge has countless meanings, so it is all about *perspective*.[10] Further, if anyone tries to make their perspective universal, they are simply exercising the "will to power"—imposing their perspective on others.

So what shapes our perspective? What determines whether the pictures we see are rabbits or ducks (and perhaps even which pictures we look at)? The media. Or more to the point, the new super-saturation of the media—what Todd Gitlin has called the "media torrent."[11] This determines what we see and what we don't, what we think about and what never enters our mind. It even shapes *how* we

think. "All media work us over completely," Marshall McLuhan warned. "They are so pervasive in their personal, political, economic, aesthetic, psychological, moral, ethical, and social consequences that they leave no part of us untouched, unaffected, unaltered."[12] Fred Fedler, author of one of the most widely used college textbooks on the mass media, writes that "the media may constitute the most powerful education system ever

Friedrich Nietzsche

known to man."[13] Supporting this contention the Public Agenda poll, conducted by the Nickelodeon cable network and a marketing and social research firm, found that today's children get more of their information about life from TV than from their parents. And the media are wildly biased, often openly so.[14]

Film director Oliver Stone, deflecting criticism for the distortions and factual errors in his films, particularly the feigned documentary exposé on the Kennedy assassination, *JFK*, once said in a lecture at American University that films shouldn't be the end-all for what is true. "[People] have a responsibility to read a book," he said. "[Nobody] is going to sit through a three-hour movie and say, 'That's that.'"[15] He's wrong. That is exactly what they do.

In the *Matrix* films, the "matrix" is an artificial world created by computers in order to immerse human minds into a false reality to keep them subdued. Humans' true lives are carried out in isolated containers for the harvesting of their bodies' energy. But the matrix

Times Square

is so complete, so all-encompassing, that it keeps their minds at bay and in full submission. The media is *our* matrix. It is not just that the communications we live among deceive; broadcast a limiting ideology; emphasize sex and violence; convey diminished images of the good, the true and the normal; corrode the quality of art; or reduce language—all of which they do. More important, they saturate our lives with the promise of meaning. Gitlin concludes that "the torrent of images, songs, and stories streaming has become our familiar world." Playing off of Marshall McLuhan's famous phrase "the medium is the message," Gitlin suggests that the "montage is the message."[16]

Our changing sense of reality is due in large part to the torrent of media becoming reality—and understanding reality in and through that torrent. Since the media do little else but present perspective, the immersion is complete. By conveying to us that everything is a matter of personal perspective, the media torrent has itself become the dominant perspective, exercising the most complete "will to power" of all.

A CHANGING VIEW OF TRUTH

So what has happened to truth? The growing idea is that there is no such thing.

Jacques Derrida, perhaps the most famous of postmodern philosophers, calls for a rampant subjectivity, even "deconstruction," of any text and its attempt to "construct" reality. For Derrida every statement not only *can* be questioned but *must* be questioned. Our understanding of reality is based on multiple images and interpretations, reconstructions and spins, circulated by the media and the marketplace. So truth is not discovered; it is *chosen*. Since everything is perspectival, Richard Rorty, another postmodern philosopher, argues that the goal is to *talk* about things, but not to arrive at any *conclusions* — "continuing a conversation rather than . . . discovering a truth."[17] Why? Truth, at least in the way it had been understood during the time of the Enlightenment, does not exist; hence it cannot be found.

The person responsible for the popular use of the term *postmodern*, Jean-François Lyotard, attempted a definition that was, by his own account, "simplifying to the extreme," yet his effort pinpointed the dynamic at hand: "I define postmodern as incredulity towards metanarratives."[18] Translation: skepticism toward any story that claims to be *the* story. According to Lyotard the main metanarrative of the modern world was the Enlightenment contention that science is the savior of the human condition. All of language and culture took second place to the pronouncements and grand vision of science. Science was the one thing that was real. Science was the one thing that was true — *the* story, *the* metanarrative. Superstitious beliefs, particularly those related to myth and religion, had been swept away.

But the growing sense is that the scientific story does not tell all there is of the tale. No story does. Old talk about a "worldview" is lost amid the sense that the very *idea* of a "worldview" is bankrupt, for no single view is able to speak to the entire world. The postmodern tendency is to embrace the narratives of particular peoples and celebrate the diversity and plurality of the world without attempting to discover a single, grand scheme into which all of the stories fit.[19]

This is radically different than Enlightenment thinking, which believed deeply in universal truth — just that it could only be found through the senses (as opposed to tradition or revelation) and therefore was reduced to what the senses could discover. The Enlightenment problem with the Christian faith was not that it wasn't true, only that it could not be empirically verified. The Enlightenment charge was never that truth *itself* did not exist. The postmodern problem with faith is not that it might be false but that it dares to lay claim to being true. If the Enlightenment bias was that humans could know everything, the postmodern disposition is that we can't know *anything*.

THE SEARCH FOR THE SPIRITUAL

So where does this leave the soul? Empty — but at least sensing it.

The founder of Harvard University's department of sociology, Pitirim Sorokin, argued that the pendulum of civilization generally swings in one of two directions: the "ideational" and the "sensate." Ideational cultures are those that are ascetic in nature, focusing on the transformation of someone's *inner* life. Sensate cultures, on the other hand, are materialistic and are based on the improvement and modification of the *outer* world. Thus the ideational civilization is more theological and spiritual, and the sensate world is more rational or scientific. Sorokin contended that the classic ideational period was the medieval. From the Enlightenment forward, we have lived in a sensate world. Now, in our struggle with what the modern world has given to us — or more accurately, taken away — there seems to be a swing back toward the ideational. We are rediscovering the validity of faith, once again making room for insight, intuition and even revelation.[20] Articles on angels, near-death experiences, prayer and healing have become cover stories. Spiritual themes run throughout contemporary music. Films and television increasingly explore religious ideas and settings. People are interested in spiritual things, they're asking spiritual questions, and they are beginning to see that many of their deepest needs are spiritual in nature.

Detroit sportswriter Mitch Albom spoke to this in his poignant collection of conversations with a dying mentor, *Tuesdays with Morrie*. Morrie Schwartz had been both professor and friend to Albom. Accidentally stumbling on his former teacher's fight with Lou Gehrig's disease, Mitch reunites with Morrie and begins meeting with him on Tuesdays to talk of life and death, purpose and meaning. Coming face-to-face with his dying instructor forces Albom to look at his own life:

> *What happened to me?* I asked myself. Morrie's high, smoky voice took me back to my university years, when I thought rich people were evil, a shirt and tie were prison clothes, and life without freedom to get up and go—motorcycle beneath you, breeze in your face, down the streets of Paris, into the mountains of Tibet—was not a good life at all. *What happened to me?* The eighties happened. The nineties happened. Death and sickness and getting fat and going bald happened. I traded lots of dreams for a bigger paycheck, and I never even realized I was doing it.

But then Morrie himself addresses what happened to Mitch—or perhaps what *needed* to happen. As the relationship between Albom and his dying mentor deepened, Morrie felt the freedom to tell Mitch that the things he had been spending so much time on, such as his work, may not have been so important. "You might have to make room for some more spiritual things," Morrie counsels Mitch. And then his old professor plunges in: "You hate that word, don't you? 'Spiritual.' You think it's touchy-feely stuff. . . . Mitch, even I don't know what 'spiritual development' really means. But I do know we're deficient in some way. We are too involved in materialistic things, and they don't satisfy us."[21] Albom proved receptive, as increasing numbers in our world today are. Douglas Coupland expresses it well:

> Here's my secret: I tell it to you with an openness of heart that I
> doubt I shall ever achieve again, so I pray that you are in a quiet
> room as you hear these words. My secret is that I need God—
> that I am sick and can no longer make it alone. I need God to
> help me give, because I no longer seem to be capable of giving;
> to help me be kind, as I no longer seem capable of kindness; to
> help me love, as I seem beyond being able to love.[22]

So we live in a day that is more open to spiritual things than ever.
Yet in light of pluralization, along with the increasing skepticism toward a single story for all of reality and reality itself considered a matter of personal perspective, it is spirituality that people are engaging,
not religion. There is a keenly felt emptiness resulting from a secularized, materialistic world that has led to a hunger for something
more, but many are unable to go further than the search for a spiritual *experience*. Postmoderns have found that the soul cannot be de-
nied, but all they know to do is search for something "soulish." From
this has come a mystic's approach to spiritual reality. It's a secularism
that is best described, to use a phrase from Christopher Dawson, as
"religious emotion divorced from religious belief."[23] Belief doesn't
matter, just symbol, feeling and image. So while pollsters contend
that high percentages of the U.S. population claims to believe in
God, James Herrick notes that the nature of that divinity is defined
in widely divergent ways. Instead there is a "new religious synthesis"
that holds to an unsettling combination of Christian orthodoxy,
Eastern mysticism, New Age belief and the occult.[24]

Little wonder that a department store Christmas display had no
difficulty featuring Santa Claus nailed to a cross.[25]

FROM THE POSTMODERN TO THE POSTHUMAN

In Lewis Carroll's beloved classic *Alice's Adventures in Wonderland*, young Alice encounters a large caterpillar sitting on a mushroom and smoking a pipe.

"Who are *you?*" said the Caterpillar.

"I—I hardly know, sir, just at present—at least I know who I *was* when I got up this morning, but I think I must have been changed several times since then."

"What do you mean by that?" said the Caterpillar sternly. "Explain yourself!"

"I can't explain *myself*, I'm afraid, sir," said Alice, "because I'm not myself, you see."[26]

In an insane world where reality and truth no longer existed, Lewis Carroll insightfully imagined that his Alice in "wonderland" would quickly lose any sense of personal identity as well. His imagination proved prophetic.

One of the great questions in all of human thought is *Who am I?* The answer is fast becoming *I don't know.* Humanism made human beings the measure of all things. The dilemma is that we no longer know what it means to *be* human. As Connie Zweig has noted, the very idea of self is under siege. "In much the same way that Nietzsche's pronouncement that 'God is dead' reverberated . . . a parallel declaration of the death of the Self troubles our own time."[27] If human beings have no fixed or permanent essence, if we are "plastic"—subject through technology to alteration, enhancement, mutation, control—then we may do what we will with ourselves. And so we have.

Ernest Trova's *Wheel Man*

The result is not a utopia of perfect bodies and healthy psyches, much less a new sense of identity. Instead, it is more along the lines of Ernest Trova's *Wheel Man*, a dehumanized, life-sized bronze figure of no particular age, sex, race, culture or environment. Compressed between two wheels, it pictures a humanity able to create incredible wonders through technology, but in so doing, devaluing humanity itself. With apt symbolism Trova reveals how the wheels of human progress do not always carry the human race to greater happiness, much less to a deeper sense of identity. As C. S. Lewis forecast in a prescient 1947 essay, "Man's final conquest has proved to be the abolition of man."[28]

CRYING IN THE NIGHT

Frederick Buechner tells of a boy of twelve or thirteen who, in a fit of crazy anger and depression, got ahold of a gun and killed his father. When the authorities asked the boy why he had done it, he said it was because he could not stand his father because he demanded too much of the boy, because his father was always after him, because he hated his father. Later, after he had been placed in a house of detention, a guard was walking down the corridor late one night when he heard sounds from the boy's room, and he stopped to listen. The words that he heard the boy sobbing out in the dark were "I want my father, I want my father."[29]

We live in a day of peril and promise. The spiral of history from the Middle Ages to the Enlightenment has been downward in many ways; the cultural currents of secularization, privatization and pluralization have undermined much of the context for faith; the world which now lives in us—often Christian and non-Christian alike—is far from that envisioned by Christ for the world he came to save. Yet the serious nature of our day holds promise. Buechner observes that the story of the boy is a kind of parable of the lives of all of us. We have killed off our Father and now feel the emptiness it brings. We are now looking for comfort in a renewed search for an identity as sons and daughters.[30]

If only those who *are* sons and daughters would show the way.

COME AND WALK
AMONG US:
THE LIFE OF ST. PATRICK

It was a pagan world, outside the borders
of the accepted disciplines and understandings of civilization. But it was spiritual, deeply spiritual. The supernatural
was everywhere, in places and days, people and events, filling their
lives with images, symbols and ritual. The earth and all in it were sacred; gods and goddesses roamed the landscape; the world of magic
was embraced, but there was no God who sat in heaven and no
knowledge of a Christ who had come to earth.

Into this postmodern milieu, fifteen hundred years before postmodernism was born, came Patrick, the patron saint and national
apostle of Ireland (c. fifth century).

Patrick did not come to his task by choice. Kidnapped at the age
of fifteen from his father's villa in Britain, he was enslaved in Ireland
and made to serve as a shepherd. There he came into the fullness of
Christian faith, and after six years of praying he finally made his escape. But on reaching his homeland, he had a dream where a man
who seemed to come from Ireland handed him a letter titled "The
Voice of the Irish," and at the same time heard the voices of those
who lived "beside the Wood of Foclut, which lies near the Western
Sea" asking him to "come back and walk once more among us."
Patrick writes that he was "pierced to my heart's core."[1]

Patrick returned to Ireland—not as a slave but as a missionary.

The legends surrounding Patrick are, well, legendary. He report-
edly drove the snakes of Ireland into the sea. Whether true or not,
there are no snakes in Ireland to this day. Another is that he used the
shamrock to explain the Trinity. There may be some truth to this;

pointing back to Patrick, the shamrock is the national flower of Ireland. He is to have confronted and overpowered the druids, fasted for forty days and nights on a holy mountain, and openly challenged a king by lighting a fire for an Easter celebration in open opposition to the edict that only one fire was to burn in the land, and that for the pagan feast of Beltane.

What is true is that Patrick looked for ways to connect the message of Christ to a pagan, supernatural world. In doing so, he imaginatively put himself in the position of the Irish. Looking for what they held in common, Patrick made clear that he too embraced a world full of magic. The difference between Patrick's magic and the magic of the druids was that in Patrick's world "all beings and events come from the hand of a good God."[2] When Patrick arrived, the Irish were still practicing human sacrifice; Patrick made it clear that through Christ's supreme sacrifice such offerings were no longer needed. Patrick took an entire culture's leanings toward the spiritual and led them to Christ.

During Patrick's time all who lived outside of the boundaries, or walls, of Rome were called "barbarians" and were to be avoided at all costs. The Irish were barbarians. Thomas Cahill writes that Patrick was the first Christian missionary to a culture outside of Rome's world: "The step he took was in its way as bold as Columbus's." Patrick simply wrote, "I came in God's strength . . . and had nothing to fear."[3] As a result, Patrick "not only changed the course of Irish history but made Ireland the burning and shining light of barbarian Europe for the best part of the next thousand years."[4]

INTERLUDE

"I see no reason why the decay of culture
should not proceed much further."

T. S. ELIOT

Søren Kierkegaard wrote of a fire that broke out backstage in a theater. The clown came out to inform the audience. They thought it was just part of the show—a joke—and applauded his announcement. He repeated his warning, but they shouted all the louder.

Kierkegaard concludes, "So I think the world will come to an end amid general applause from all the wits, who believe that it is a joke."[1]

But the demise of the world is not a joke. It is the challenge of our day, and responding as Christ followers is the great call on our lives. The serious nature of our day has presented us with a *kairos* moment—how we live and act in response takes on new meaning and urgency.[2] *Kairos* is time filled with opportunity, a moment pregnant with eternal significance and possibility. In the book of Jeremiah, Pharaoh is said to be only a loud noise and nothing more, because he had missed such a moment (Jer 46:17). In the New Testament Jesus talks about specific times of testing that will determine faith's final outcome for all who receive the word of God (Lk 8:13).[3] "Nothing is more critical than to recognize and respond to such a moment," writes Os Guinness. "Before will hardens into fate and choice into 'might have been,' the *[kairos]* hour is the moment when the present is at its greatest intensity and the future is uniquely open to our decision and action."[4] But how to live? How to respond?

H. Richard Niebuhr outlined the many responses that could be made in light of the interplay between Christ and culture.[5] Some react in anger and hostility, emphasizing the opposition between

Christ and culture. Historically, this has often meant retreat rather than engagement. At the opposite end of the spectrum would be those who survey the cultural landscape and feel that there is—or should be—a fundamental agreement between Christ and culture, so Christ is continually recast in the guise of culture's predominant values in order to represent the pinnacle of human achievement. Rather than Christ standing over and against culture as judge and challenger, Christ is absorbed into the culture and appropriated for its ends, making Christ little more than a reflection of culture itself.

A third alternative stands against both a Christ *against* and a Christ *of* culture. Christ the *transformer* of culture.

But for Christ to become the transformer of culture, he needs transformed lives through which to work. Jesus initiated the great revolution through the cross, then he entrusted the message of the cross to men and women. They were not particularly educated, sophisticated, wealthy or influential, but that was not what was most needed. Engagement with the world demanded one thing—that they be like *him*. The heart of Jesus' strategy for transforming the world was unleashing a force of transformed lives.

This is how the world will be changed: individuals who have had their lives touched by Christ turning around and touching the lives of others. Thomas Kelly writes that we are first torn loose from earthly attachments and ambitions and then quickened to a divine concern for the world. "He plucks the world out of our hearts. . . . And He hurls the world into our hearts, where we and He together carry it in infinitely tender love."[6] It is not that pursuing cultural agendas through various political or social processes is unimportant. But a Christian nation is not forged primarily through legislation. And a Christian nation is not even the first goal, as if the mission is to steer culture toward some form of theocracy. The primary goal is a nation of Christians, which can then shape the heart of a nation toward Christian values.

But what kind of Christian will this take? The world is full of Christ followers—committed ones—particularly in the United States. Yet the tide does not seem to be turning.

I have wrestled with this question my entire Christian life. Is it something we are? Is it about how we live? How we think? Our action? The answer is, of course, yes. It is all of these things, but more. Yet such questions often miss the larger journey. Ignited by a sense of the serious nature of our times and the inescapable call to do something in and for Christ in response, I must look comprehensively at my life. I must begin with certain investments, basic preparations that enlarge my capacities. From this I can be developed and matured, strengthened and made ready. Then there must come a conscious, intentional positioning that situates my life for action. There are key outposts where I must station myself. From such places I can act, respond and be used by the living God.

But what is to be developed? I return again and again to two areas: my mind and my soul. And the outposts I must fill? It would be hard to miss the front lines of kingdom advance: my vocation in the world and my place in the body of Christ, the church. Added to this must come a singular concern—the sharing of Christ with the world in such a way that the lost are found, the blind see, the deaf hear and the hurting comforted. I must *understand* that the world is in desperate need of Christ and become passionate about being his ambassador.

With humility and insight Ralph Wood reveals the need for such convictions. Fresh out of graduate study at the University of Chicago, Wood writes of embarking on his first year in the classroom as a professor. One spring afternoon a knock on his door came from a student taking his class on theology and modern literature. The student asked if his girlfriend could join them. The student explained that they were on their way to the airport where the girl would take a flight to New York for an abortion. This was 1972, a year before *Roe v. Wade,* so it would also be a criminal act.

"We want to know what you have to say to us."

"I had approached my first year of teaching believing that my chief task was to wipe the grins off fundamentalist faces," Wood recalls. "I wanted to sophisticate my students by rubbing their pious noses in the crusty snows of secularity, challenging what I assumed to be their firm but naïve faith by confronting them with the hard quandaries of modern unbelief." But he was made painfully aware of the limits of such an agenda on that fateful day. His student made it clear—as so many subsequent students would as well—that he and his girlfriend possessed so little faith that there was almost nothing to challenge, much less to overthrow. "What they needed was not sophistication . . . but edification and instruction of the most fundamental kind."

Wood writes that he wished there was a happy ending. There was not. He did not dissuade them from aborting the baby. He did not point them toward a Christian community that would not be scandalized by illegitimacy. He did not involve his own congregation in helping the young woman give birth to the child and then put it up for adoption. He did not convince them to marry and nurture the child themselves.

> Instead, I backed and filled and stammered and fumbled, making inane claims about God's grace and mercy. Having looked to me for the bread of life, this young man and woman received little more than a stone. I had been teaching as if it didn't matter, and when the time came for it really to matter, I was found wanting in the worst way.[7]

But he is not alone. Far too many of us have been living as if our faith didn't matter. We stroll casually through the years as if how we live and what we offer to others through our life are largely irrelevant, separate from the front lines of kingdom advance. But it's not. *Everything* rests on our lives. Peter Kreeft notes that the deepest reason why the church is weak and the world is decaying at its alarming rate is that there are not enough saints. Then he adds, "No, that's not quite honest. The reason is that *we* are not saints."[8]

But we can be.

The word *saint* means "those who are set apart," someone who is no longer part of this world but is *against* it—and as a result *for* its reclamation. Those who come to God through Christ have been declared such beings. Our life journey is meant to unfold as a series of steps toward becoming who God has declared us to be.

We must deepen our souls, allowing a wellspring of the living water of God to surface, and as a result we will have something to offer the world that it does not already have.

We must develop our minds so that we can engage the prevailing worldviews that assault the citadels of faith—not simply to defend Christianity but to be able to present Christianity as a winsome and compelling alternative.

We must respond to God's call in such a way as to fulfill our place in this world and then fill it full with the aroma and agenda of Christ.

We must align ourselves with the church so that we position ourselves in the heat of the battle and number ourselves among the vanguard of armies.

"I am Culture," a webzine once suggested. "I am the art in your arthouses, the ideas in your institutions, the laws in your land, the message in your movies, the thoughts of your teachers, the reason in your religion, the values that you value. I affect you. Do you affect me?"[9]

It is to this challenge that we now turn.

DEEPENING OUR SOULS

"Out in front of us is the drama of individuals and of nations, seething, struggling, laboring, dying. Upon this tragic drama in these days our eyes are all set in anxious watchfulness and in prayer. But within the silences of human souls an eternal drama is ever being enacted, in these days as well as in others. And on the outcomes of this inner drama rest, ultimately, the outer pageant of history."

THOMAS R. KELLY

"Everybody thinks of changing humanity and nobody thinks of changing himself."

LEO TOLSTOY

The spiritual life is first of all a *life*."¹ These words from Thomas Merton remind me that my spiritual life is not something merely to be talked about or studied but to be lived. The spiritual life is "the increasing vitality and sway of God's Spirit in us," writes Marjorie J. Thompson. "It is a magnificent choreography of the Holy Spirit in the human spirit."² Yet not many of us enter the dance.

We are more like the HBO character Tony Soprano, who along with the rest of his Mafia friends and family members is a blazing mixture of good and bad, normal and abnormal, loving family and hurting them, being loyal and selfish, spiritual yet profoundly hypocritical. Writ large in Shakespearean fashion, we resonate deeply with such characters. I know I do.

In his book on the *Sopranos* television series, Chris Seay pointed out something that I had missed in my own viewing. Throughout the series, hanging around Tony's neck, is a gold chain bearing a pendant of Saint Jerome. Jerome, an Italian, was born 342 years after the birth of Jesus. Jerome neglected his faith, sowing his wild oats and living a life very much like Tony. But then in a life-changing dream Jerome sat before the judgment seat of God.

God asked him, "Who are you?"

Jerome replied, "A Christian."

But God corrected him, saying "You are a liar. You are not a Christian."

The realization was painful, but it changed Jerome's life. He went on to become a great translator of the Bible and a leader of the church. The question throughout the *Sopranos* is whether Tony will ever see himself under the same light of truth. In what may have been the best episode of the first season, Tony takes his daughter on a trip up the East Coast for a series of college visits. Just normal father-daughter time. During the trip he spots someone who used to be part of the mob, then turned informant, who had been living under a witness protection program. Suddenly Tony the father becomes Tony the hunter—and eventual executioner. Leaving his daughter at one of her college interviews, he sneaks off, gun in hand, to commit murder. At the end of the episode the hypocrisy of it all is caught in a short but profound moment. Tony escorts his daughter to another interview. As he patiently waits outside of the office, he glances up and sees a quote from Nathaniel Hawthorne written on the hallway wall: "No man can wear one face to himself and another to the multitude without finally getting bewildered as to which may be true."

In a single moment, Tony comes face to face with the hypocrisy of his life.

And as millions of us watched, so did we.

SEEKING THE FACE OF GOD

The world will only be changed when those who call themselves Christians begin to follow Christ, becoming scandalously present in the world in all of their Christlike particularity. Such a life is a formidable presence, forever marking everything in its wake—or not.

When I first went to college, I considered myself a Christian, but there was little of my life given over to Christ's leadership, much less developed in intimacy. In truth, I pursued a life radically separated from him. My freshman roommate was a Mormon, and I recall one night—after more than a few beers—talking with him about the inadequacies of his faith when he took a dagger and drove it into my soul: "Jim, how can you say anything at all about my faith with the way you live?"

There was nothing I could say. In truth, I wasn't a Christ follower. In time, I would be. It would have little to do with beer but everything to do with my relationship with Christ and the degree to which I would allow that relationship to impact my life. I had to learn a simple truth: To live *for* God, we must live *with* God.

But what does this mean?

The answer rests in the goal of all spiritual formation, which is to be marked by the fruit of the Spirit—such things as love, joy, peace, patience, kindness, gentleness, self-control. But the fruit of the Spirit is just that. *Fruit.* The metaphor is important. Fruit does not exist in and of itself. It is something that is *produced.* It comes from a life source—a branch or a vine. A person does not *decide* to be patient, much less *will* to be patient. Patience must be cultivated from the *source* of patience. That is why the Bible speaks of such things flowing from the Spirit. They emanate from a life with, in and through the Spirit. Only when a spiritual life is cultivated will spiritual fruit be manifest. The true goal of spiritual formation is not the fruit of the Spirit but the relational intimacy that *produces* the fruit of the Spirit.

So, is deepening the soul and becoming a spiritual person just about answering the command to "love God"? *Of course.*

But that is the problem. "We have heard the words so often that we no longer hear them," reflects Frederick Buechner. "They are too loud to hear, too big to take in. We know the words so much *by* heart that we scarcely know them any longer as words spoken *to* the heart out of a mystery beyond all knowing."[3] But it runs deeper—we have made love for God tame. An intimate relationship with God has become something subtly woven into the deepest recesses of our private life instead of a reckless love bursting out of the seams of our soul, exploding into the world around us. We must recapture the words relating to love and relationship with God anew, and through them carve out a still point for our souls to absorb it all.

This is why throughout the Scriptures, particularly in the cavernous devotional spaces of the Psalms, the recurring theme is pursuing an intimate relationship with God. After the initial throes of romance, love is not a state as much as a pursuit, something tended, nurtured, *developed.* In the simple but profound words of the psalmist, we are enjoined to "Look to the Lord and his strength; seek his face always" (Ps 105:4). We should not let the brevity of the words lessen their impact—the most sensitive of souls have been profoundly shaped by their weight. This short verse is cited four times in Augustine's *The Trinity.* Historian Robert Louis Wilken notes that "more than any other passage in the Bible [Psalm 105] captures the spirit of the early Christian thinking."[4] Yet most of us do not seek the face of God.

The impact of most Christ followers on this world is minimal because the degree to which we seek intimacy with Christ is minimal. When there is little that reflects a relationship with Christ in us, we have little of Christ to offer. I know that I have had opportunities when I could have made an impact, but I had little to give, all because of spiritual anemia. There was more of *this* world than the world *to come* coursing through my veins. But we need not starve our souls or allow our relationship with God through Christ to fade like the dying embers of an untended fire. We *can seek* the face of God. But how?

William Law (1686-1761) was a spiritual director whose devotees track record was nothing less than historic: the Gibbon family, including Edward Gibbon, author of the famed *The Decline and Fall of the Roman Empire*; the legendary lexicographer Samuel Johnson; John Henry Newman, leader of the Oxford Movement; and the founder of Methodism, John Wesley. Obviously Law was a man who took advantage of the investment opportunities God brought his way. His most famous treatise contains his secret in its title: *A Serious Call to a Devout and Holy Life*. To seek God's face is a serious call, one which is to be engaged with utmost earnestness.

This raises the real question, offered most simply by the Quaker writer Douglas Steere: How does a person become increasingly Christian when he or she already is one?[5] The answer throughout Christian history has seldom wavered: *Live the life that Jesus lived.*

"We can . . . become like Christ," writes Dallas Willard, "by practicing the types of activities he engaged in, by arranging our whole lives around the activities he himself practiced in order to remain constantly at home in the fellowship of his Father." Willard uses an example of an all-star baseball player who is our idol. We want to pitch and run and hit as well as he does, so in our softball league games we take the stance that he takes, hold the bat as he does and wear his brand of shoes. From this we expect to perform as he does. And, of course, we don't. "The star performer himself didn't achieve his excellence by trying to behave in a certain way only during the game," observes Willard. "Instead, he chose an overall life of preparation of mind and body."[6]

Christ calls us to this kind of discipline in order to answer his call to our world.

Yet there are few spiritual athletes. We are weak, flabby and out of shape. Our lives have become earthly in orientation and fleshly in operation. We conform to the patterns of the world, when we could be morphed into the very image of Christ (Rom 12:1-2). We focus on religion instead of relationship. Practice instead of passion. Such a life—not rooted in an authentic relationship with God, full of rhetoric and posturing, form and mannerism—is all but empty. We become people possessed with knowledge "about" as opposed to an acquaintance "with." But only intimate relationship with the living God leads to true spirituality. And only true spirituality can affect the world.

So how do we live *with* and *like* Christ? Two thousand years of spiritual history have spoken with a single voice: the reading and study of God's Word, obedience, prayer, silence and solitude, and some form of spiritual direction; these are the investments and practices that, time and again, have led men and women to true spirituality.

But who am I to write of such things? Trust me, I feel this more deeply than you, and so do others. "It is true, my dear reader," confessed Francis de Sales (1567-1622), the great spiritual director who was declared a saint by Pope Alexander VII in 1665, "that I write about the devout life although I myself am not devout."[7] But what I sense fueled Francis de Sales, and I know fuels most on this journey, is not a sense of having "arrived" but a personal hunger. Speaking for myself, I do not feel that I have cultivated a model spiritual life, but I know that it is a spiritual life that I most want. It is from the depths of the soul that a life most clearly and significantly speaks, and makes its mark and is able to bring Christ to bear on the world. Any life-giving water I might offer to those who thirst is drawn from the well of my soul.

But there lies the rub. I say I hunger for this, but do I? In truth, I don't always want to go deep. It is easier—far easier—to live my life on the surface waters of communion with God. Going deep with God, as with anyone, is demanding, difficult, time-consuming; it calls for intentionality and discipline, purpose and drive. Like most, I know there is *more*, but I have often found myself to be inconsistent—or unwilling—in the effort.

This is the problem.

"Superficiality is the curse of our age," writes Richard J. Foster. "The doctrine of instant satisfaction is a primary spiritual problem. The desperate need today is not for a greater number of intelligent people, or gifted people, but for deep people."[8] This is what Thomas Kelly wrote so profoundly of in *A Testament of Devotion*, noting that we are to live life on two levels: the level of hurried activity and then the life of the interior world. The dilemma is that many of us only choose to inhabit the first level. The frantic race through life becomes the only plane of existence in which we operate or from which we draw.[9] It is a very shallow well.

KNOWING GOD

When we are ready to dig deeper, seeking God's face first requires us to first hear his voice. Spiritual formation looks first to the Scriptures because it is through revelation that God speaks to us and makes himself known. Henri Nouwen once asked John Eudes, his spiritual director during his seven-month stay in a Trappist monastery, "When I pray, to whom do I pray?" and "When I say 'Lord,' what do I mean?" Eudes responded, "This is the real question, this is the most important question you can raise; at least this is the question that you can make your most important question."[10]

The Bible is not merely a book. It is the very Word of God, living and active. There is a dynamic interplay between its pages and our lives. Many Christians are adept at biblical study: we have our dictionaries and concordances, study Bibles and small group curricula. Yet Simon Chan notes that spiritual reading "is concerned with the Bible as the Word of God that calls us to God."[11] This is not my tendency when I read. I read for information, not reflection. I look for facts, not encounter. My natural inclination is to engage my mind, but not my heart—and certainly not my soul. Granted, God often invades my inner recesses without warning, for his Word is sharper than any double-edged sword, but that is far different than creating the space for an encounter to take place and actively inviting him in. Simply waiting for such moments to happen borders on presumption and does not actively cultivate the inner life I need.

Ken Gire has written that to read the Word without taking time to reflect on it would be like sitting at a table where a sumptuous meal has been prepared and eyeing all the food but never eating. And to reflect on the Word without prayerfully responding to it would be like chewing the food but never swallowing.[12] Spiritual reading is "reflective and prayerful," reminds Marjorie J. Thompson. "It is concerned not with speed or volume but with depth and receptivity. That is because the purpose of spiritual reading is to open ourselves to how God may be speaking to us in and through any particular text."[13]

This is actually a very ancient practice known as *lectio divina* that was once common among Christians. The idea was to read the Bible slowly, contemplatively, to allow the Scriptures to penetrate and afford a union with God. Our thoughts with his, our heart with his. As Benedict suggested in the prologue to his rule, the goal is to hear "with the ear of your heart,"[14] to attune ourselves to the "gentle whisper" of the word of the Lord (1 Kings 19:12). Like dry, hardened soil, I need to let the Word of God gently rain on my parched soul so that I am able to soak in every drop. This has meant less volume but more life change. The goal is not speed-reading but listening. It is being like Mary, who "pondered in her heart" all that she had seen and heard of Christ (Lk 2:19). The process is simple, but it takes enormous intent: We listen deeply by reading from the Scriptures; we meditate on what we have read in such a way that it interacts with the deepest parts of who we are; we pray through what we are hearing so that it is *applied* to the deepest parts of who we are; and finally, through contemplation we "rest in the presence of the One who has used His word as a means of inviting us to accept His transforming embrace."[15]

PRAYER

Prayer is the foundation of intimacy with God, the "inward movement" that we make toward God. Thomas Merton broadens this vision by writing that prayer "means yearning for the simple presence of God, for a personal understanding of his word, for knowledge of his will and for capacity to hear and obey him." Sharing this vision, Geoffrey Wainwright maintains that spirituality is nothing less than the "combination of prayer and living."[16] All I know is that when I pray, I draw near to God. When I don't, my soul and spirit drift far, far away.

The purpose of the ancient monastic movement—the opus Dei—was to create a life of prayer as the "work of God," that act whereby we "place God upon our heart."[17] Scripture may be the foundation of the relationship itself, for it is through revelation that this God is named and known, but intimacy with this revealed God is gained through the "presence" that comes in an act of prayer. As Quaker writer Douglas Steere has written: "It is not that he is not present at other times but that by this voluntary act of ours, the act of prayer, we are enabled to break with our outer preoccupations and to become aware of the presence and of what that presence does to search and to transform and to renew us and to send us back into life again."[18]

But this is difficult. Teresa of Ávila, a saint who has taught so many about prayer, confessed, "Very often I was more occupied with the wish to see the end of my hour for prayer. I used to actually watch the sandglass. And the sadness that I sometimes felt on entering my prayer-chapel was so great that it required all my courage to force myself inside."[19] I know how she felt.

Teresa of Ávila

But prayer is not meant to be an experience driven event. If it were, I know that I would be extremely frustrated and greatly discouraged. I doubt I would pray as often as I do. Instead, prayer is *relationship* driven. I pray because I am in a relationship with God in Christ through the Holy Spirit, and apart from prayer I would not have much of a relationship. I enter into communication, conversation and communion with God through prayer. It's when I lay out the pieces of my life on God's altar, and when he then returns them to me anew (Ps 5:3).

So, like many others, I come to God daily for prayer. Often empty, often having to woodenly plod through prayer using the acrostic ACTS (Adoration, Confession, Thanksgiving, Supplication) as my soul often needs help to find its way, I tell God I love him and offer him praise for who he is; I confess my sins—specifically, graphically—as my mind scrolls through the day before; I thank God for all that I have been given, acknowledging that every good and perfect gift comes from above; and I ask him for help—to intervene, to provide, to come to my rescue. And it matters.

I have found that prayer, no matter how dry, forced or mechanical it might be, opens my life to a longer conversation and communication with God throughout the day. It is as if my morning prayer invites him into the flow of things and sets him prominently in the forefront of my thoughts and feelings. From this I am able to engage the world I live in—and which lives in me—with a transcendent mooring instead of a temporal one. My inner world is transformed, for it is wrenched away from life lived on the hurried, frantic level of activity and thrust into the eternity of soul and spirit. There God speaks, corrects, reminds, renews. I then find myself able to walk through the world with sharpened eyes, increased sensitivity to the Spirit's promptings, heightened insight and deepened wisdom. Even more, when I have come to God in prayer and have asked him to infuse my life with his power and provision, I tap into the resources of heaven itself. Apart from this, I can do nothing.

SILENCE AND SOLITUDE

In his catalog of wisdom from the desert fathers of the fourth century, Thomas Merton tells of a certain brother who went to Abbot Moses in Scete and asked him for a good word. The elder said to him, "Go, sit in your cell, and your cell will teach you everything."[20]

The power of silence and solitude has been recognized throughout the history of spiritual formation. It is the purposeful separation of ourselves from the world in order to place ourselves with God. The evil one assaults our senses with the material world to drown out the distant chords of eternity's symphony. Only in silence can we move past the deafening roar of the world and hear the music of God.

Here it is important to remember the difference between spiritual quietness and the mere absence of sound that creates silence. "Silence is the absence of sound and quiet the stilling of sound," writes Frederick Buechner. "Quiet chooses to be silent. It holds its breath to listen."[21] The rule of St. Benedict speaks of *cultivating* silence in our lives.

To gain this silence requires a companion discipline: *solitude.* Though often marked by physical isolation, the goal is not so much a place as it is a state of mind, one where there is—in the ancient Celtic sense—an "inner attentiveness to God" alone.[22] But we are physical creatures living in space and time. As a result, space and time affects us in ways we seldom imagine. Solitude provides the necessary separation from our environment that affords objectivity and fresh awareness of the deepest realities and priorities of life.

Drawing again from the Celtic tradition, these become our "thin places," with the accompanying "thin times." The Celts believed that the other world was always close to us, but that it was during these times and places that we were alone with God that the veil was lifted and the other world became apparent.[23]

But silence, not to mention the solitude necessary to bring it to life, does not naturally present itself. These times and spaces must be *created*, beginning with a daily time with God. Often called devotions, or quiet times, these daily withdrawals form the basis for the solitude on which a spiritually formed life is founded. From such times we should "gather a little devotional bouquet," suggests Francis de Sales. He was referring to how, when walking through a gar-

Celtic cross

den, it is not uncommon to gather into our hands four or five flowers to smell and keep for the rest of the day. "In the same way, when our soul has carefully considered by meditation a certain mystery we should select one, two, or three points that we liked best and that are most adapted to our improvement, think frequently about them, and smell them spiritually during the rest of the day."[24]

Alongside this daily discipline, E. Glenn Hinson suggests that we need an all-day retreat at least once a month. Then, perhaps twice a year, a longer withdrawal of thirty-six to forty-eight hours is needed. Finally, regardless of profession, we need annual sabbaticals.[25]

In my own life, the daily retreat has been long established, rising early in the morning for prayer and reflection, sitting by a window gazing into the early morning dawn. But I knew it wasn't enough; it barely kept my soul afloat in the teeth of life's demands. Then several years ago, within the context of a mentoring relationship, a man asked me, "Jim, what do you do that really puts gas back into your tanks? If you could do one thing that would rejuvenate you spiritually and emotionally, what would it be?"

I didn't have to pause. I knew the answer. "I would go to the mountains and be alone."

For as long as I can remember, the mountains have held a significance for my spirit and emotions that I can't explain. Being there alone is particularly rich.

He said, "Good. You should do that once a month."

I laughed. "You've got to be kidding. Once a month? The mountains? I don't have the time! My life is too busy, too full, to put something like that into my schedule.

Then he said something I will not soon forget. "If you don't, you will end up in a ditch. You will burn out, lose your ministry, perhaps even your family, and become a casualty of the cause." I knew he was right. I saw the edges of my life fraying and knew how easily my world could unravel. I went to the mountains.

My first trip found me staying in a budget hotel, just overnight, in the heart of the Blue Ridge. I remember it to this day. It was like water in a dry desert. I felt energy and emotional renewal flowing into the deepest recesses of my inner being. I came home walking on air. I entered our foyer, hugged my kids and kissed my wife; she thought I had been drinking. I had—from the well of renewal that God intends for all of us to take deep draughts of living water.

Now I escape monthly to a little bed and breakfast in the mountains. I leave on a Thursday afternoon, and as I drive toward the clean air and clear skies, I feel the weight of the world fall off my shoulders. As soon as I arrive, I take a hike deep into the Blue Ridge and regain the bearings of my life. I pray. I sing. I weep. I *feel.* Returning to my room, I read and reflect, journal and pray. I gaze over a seventy-mile vista. It is nothing less than the richest possible time with God. I feast off of it for weeks. Four, to be exact. Then I venture to my precious mountains once again. On the front end I would have told you that it was impossible to put this into my life. Looking back, it is unthinkable not to have it.

Not everyone has the ability to travel to the mountains once a month, but the practice of retreat itself is open to all. A solitary moment before dawn, a walk in a nearby park, a bench in a quiet garden. We can all withdraw daily, and if needed, find the means to escape for longer periods. Doing so allows us to return to the world with a fullness of spirit that offsets the emptiness of the world around us.

SPIRITUAL DIRECTION

"Do you seriously wish to travel the road to devotion?" asked Francis de Sales. "If so, look for a good man to guide and lead you. This is the most important of all words of advice."[26] Many words have been used to describe life-on-life instruction: discipling, mentoring, coaching. The more time-honored description, and the one that points to the most compelling of the relational practices, is spiritual direction. In her writings on such matters, Jeannette Bakke notes that someone seeks a mentor to develop certain competencies. Being "discipled" often involves defined plans that the one being discipled is to follow step by step. The discipler usually functions more as teacher and does more talking than listening.[27] Spiritual direction, however, is a relationship between someone who wants to grow in the Christ life and someone who is able to direct that person on how to achieve that growth.

Such direction is found throughout the Bible—Moses to Joshua, Elijah to Elisha, Elizabeth to Mary, Paul to Timothy—and in the history of the early church. John Cassian (c. 350-435), influenced by the earliest Egyptian ascetics, put each of his novices under the care of an older monk. Benedict absorbed Cassian's practice into his famed rule. By the end of the seventh century, spiritual direction was a deep and abiding aspect of Western monasticism. With the emergence of the Dominican order of itinerant friars in 1216, spiritual direction left the monastery and entered the wider Christian world. Celtic Christians called such persons *anamchairde* (soul friends). The term refers to an intimate spiritual friendship that involved both spiritual direction and mentorship in the context of trust and love.[28]

Eugene Peterson describes spiritual direction as taking place "when two people agree to give their full attention to what God is doing in one (or both) of their lives and seek to respond in faith."[29] Spiritual directors will listen to us, help us to respond to God with greater freedom, point us to practical disciplines of spiritual growth, love us and pray for us.[30] He or she is not a counselor, therapist, guru or dictator, but a mature Christ follower who helps us discover the movement of the Holy Spirit in our life.

It can take years to find such men and women for your life, but they need not all be living. A vibrant source is the great cast of saints who have gone before us, the "cloud of witnesses" the author of He-

brews speaks of. While some see such "historical" direction as a decided disadvantage, particularly in relation to that aspect of direction
that involves discerning where God is leading, I confess that some of
my most significant spiritual directors died long before my adult life.
I have drunk deeply from the intellectual well of C. S. Lewis, been
counseled on countless occasions by Francis de Sales, allowed my
innermost feelings to be probed and prodded by Henri Nouwen,
and had the contours of my life shaped by St. Benedict. But there is
little doubt that they supplement living directors who are journeying
through life by my side.

DEVELOPING YOUR RULE

At various points I have made reference to Benedict, his "rule" and
monasticism in general. Historian Mark Noll has designated the
founding of the monastic rule of St. Benedict (c. 480-c. 550) as one
of the great "turning points" in Christian history.[31] Penned at the beginning of the sixth century, Benedict wished to write a rule, a guide
for optimal spiritual formation, that would help guide monks to holiness. Thomas Moore writes that "Every thoughtful person, no matter what his or her lifestyle may be, has a rule," meaning a pattern or
model for living.[32]

I need a rule. Something that will take the scattered, frantic activities of my life and carve out space and time for God and me to
connect, and from that to have the deepest parts of who I am
formed in Christ. I need a rule that will reach into the numbing
routines of my life, what the French often refer to as *metro, boulot,
dodo* (metro, work, sleep), and create channels that spiritual life
can flow through. The key is *discipline*. This is what a rule is—a
collected, organized set of practices we determine to follow in order to tend to our spirits and shepherd our souls. We need structure
and discipline for our spiritual lives every bit as much as we do for
every other area of life.

St. Benedict writing his *Rule*

Whatever our rule may be, it can and should be natural to our personality and developed in light of our season of life—but it must be created. If we know that we would be profoundly served by reading, praying and spending time with a soul friend, then we must work toward establishing the patterns of life that allow it.

Easy? Of course not.

To pursue my rule, I rise at 5 a.m. I would rather sleep. I retreat once a month. I would rather escape to a golf course. I seek out spiritual directors. I would prefer to seek out ESPN. Such investments are not natural for me; the natural flow of my life is *away* from discipline. If disciplines come at all, I have found that they must be *cultivated*. This means that building a rule can be overwhelming.

When I first began to pursue my life relationship with Christ, I was "discipled" as to what I needed to do: pray, read my Bible, have a daily quiet time, go to church, tithe—at the same time I was trying to stop swearing, manage my hormones and demonstrate the fruit of the Spirit. There was also the small group I was encouraged to join and the ministry I was expected to begin. I couldn't do it. I tried but failed miserably. It was too much to begin at the same time. I came perilously close to abandoning all spiritual investments because the weight of facing them all at the onset was too much to bear.

This is why a rule should be developed slowly, over time, bit by bit. It is seldom wise to attempt a regimen that includes everything you can think of doing. Think with me about how we develop a daily schedule. We say to ourselves, *Here is what I want in my life. I want to work out at the gym, have a quiet time, eat a cooked breakfast, get to work early, come home, sit down with the family for dinner, help my children with homework, read, write a letter to a friend, catch the game on TV and be in bed by ten.* We do the math and find it takes a thirty-four-hour day. We do more math, a little cutting here and there, and find that we can squeeze most of it in by rising at 4 a.m. We fill in the time blocks, set the alarm and go to bed ready for our new life to begin.

At 4:20 a.m., after we have hit the snooze button for the second time, we wonder what we were thinking. We skip the gym, settle for a toasted bagel and pray in the car on the way to work. We push on through the day, but it only gets worse. We throw in the towel by noon. It is simply too much to do at once, so we end up in defeat, going back to life as lived before. But this is not the way to build a disciplined life.

It is best to begin with *one* thing and make that one thing our only goal. Whether it is to rise at 5 a.m. or have a family meal three times a week, we should drive that single stake into the ground and do all that we can to establish its place in our life. It's often said that once a behavior is maintained for six weeks, it has become habit. And once a habit, it no longer demands the emotional, physical and mental energy needed to sustain its presence in our life. It has simply become a part of who we are. Then we rise *naturally* at 5 a.m., or we *naturally* sit down together as a family to eat a meal on Mondays, Wednesdays and Thursdays.

Once a single practice reaches this point, we are ready to add another practice to our life. And then another and another; a spiritual rule is best built over time. This also allows us to tweak and discard, add and finesse. My rule now is vastly different than what it was five years ago, and I look forward to what I hope to build into it over the next half-decade.

There are many protests to the demands of living under a rule, but in the end practices themselves are not the issue. The goal is to so seek the face of God in such a way that Christ is formed in us. By themselves the spiritual disciplines can do nothing. Richard Foster wisely reminds us, "They can only get us to the place where something can be done."[33] But that is a very important place to come to. Christ formed in us will allow us to bring Christ to the world. And it needs so much more than what it now has.

SEEKING GOD:
THE LIFE OF ST. BENEDICT

We know little of his life but much of his legacy. His investment in spiritual formation is arguably the most influential of any person in Christian history since Christ, affecting the lives of millions, not simply toward deeper devotion but through that devotion toward the alteration of society itself.

As a young man Benedict of Nursia (c. 480-547) became disgusted with the paganism he encountered while studying in Rome. He determined to live in solitude in a cave outside of the city. Even there his fame as a holy man spread throughout the region. He eventually founded a grand monastery in Monte Cassino, which exists to this day, to help others live lives full of Christ. Disciples continued to flock to him, and as a result Benedict founded twelve additional monasteries.

At Monte Cassino, Benedict wrote his rule in order to guide the growing number of monks toward greater degrees of holiness. *Regula*, Latin for "rule," referred to a pattern or model. From the monastic point of view the rule was an instrument for shaping a particular kind of life.[1] The monks were determined to be "athletes of God."

Benedict's rule begins with a single word—*Listen*—which sets the tone for all that follows. We are to listen to each other and supremely to God. From this the monastic pattern each day was built around the opus Dei (the "work of God"). Seven times a day the monks would gather in the oratory in order to say the "offices," which began after midnight with vigils, then followed at daybreak by lauds, continuing until the day ended with compline. Yet the greatest contribution for spiritual formation was *commitment*. To commit to the rule demanded a full year's probation followed by a solemn vow of obedience to the rule for the remainder of life.

We know little of Benedict's life. But as Thomas Moore has noted, this "holy man cannot have taught otherwise than as he lived."[2] Benedict influenced those around him toward Christ; in turn the collective force of their lives shaped the world around them.

Historian Mark Noll writes that "monasticism was, after Christ's commission to his disciples, the most important—and in many ways the most beneficial—institutional event in the history of Christianity. . . . Almost everything in the church that approached the highest, noblest, and truest ideals of the gospel was done either by those who had chosen the monastic way or by those who had been inspired in their Christian life by the monks."[3] Little wonder that in 1964 Pope Paul VI proclaimed Benedict the patron saint of all Europe.

DEVELOPING OUR MINDS

"Let every student be plainly instructed, and earnestly pressed, to consider well [that] the maine end of his life and studies is to know God and Jesus Christ which is eternall life, Jn. 17:3, and therefore to lay Christ in the bottome, as the only foundation of all sound knowledge and Learning."

FOUNDING MISSION STATEMENT OF
HARVARD UNIVERSITY, 1643

"To put the matter baldly, we live in a thought-world, and the thinking has gone very bad indeed."

SAUL BELLOW

Forty-two percent of American adults can't locate Japan on a world map. Nearly 15 percent can't locate the United States. Seventy million Americans do not know that Germany was our enemy in World War II. A U.S. Department of Education survey found that 50 percent of all American students were unaware of the Cold War; 60 percent had no idea of how the United States came into existence. Roughly 60 percent of the adult population of the United States has never read a book of any kind, and only 6 percent reads as much as one book a year—even when *book* is defined as a Harlequin romance or self-help manual. Only 41 percent of American teenagers can name the three branches of government. But 59 percent can name the Three Stooges.[1]

CHRISTIANS AND THE MIND

The life of the mind comes easier to some than others, but the "clos-ing" of the American mind, as Allan Bloom pointedly described it, has become legendary. Yet it goes without question that our minds form a critical part of our life, particularly for Christ followers. Jesus made it clear that our minds are integral to the life lived with God: when summarizing human devotion to God as involving heart, soul and strength, Jesus added *mind*. He wanted there to be no doubt that when contemplating the comprehensive nature of commitment our intellect would not be overlooked.

Yet as Harry Blamires reminds us, "There is no longer a Christian mind." A Christian ethic, a Christian practice, a Christian spiritual-ity, yes—but not a Christian *mind*. "As a thinking being," Blamires writes, "the modern Christian has succumbed to secularization."[2] Or as Mark Noll has dryly noted, the scandal of the evangelical mind is that there is not much of an evangelical mind.[3] Worse, there is even a bias against the intellect. Richard Hofstadter, in his Pulitzer-prize-winning book *Anti-Intellectualism in American Life*, identified "the evangelical spirit" as one of the prime sources of American anti-intel-lectualism. Hofstadter points out that for many Christians humble ig-norance is a far more noble human quality than a cultivated mind.[4]

Yet it is precisely a cultivated mind that is needed for our day. John Stott writes, "We may talk of 'conquering' the world for Christ. But what sort of 'conquest' do we mean? Not a victory by force of arms. . . . This is a battle of ideas."[5] This was the concern of the apos-tle Paul, who reminded the Corinthian church that "we do not wage war as the world does. . . . We demolish arguments and every preten-sion that sets itself up against the knowledge of God, and we take captive every thought to make it obedient to Christ" (2 Cor 10:3-5).

The devaluation of the intellect is a recent development within the annals of Christian history. While Christians have long struggled with the role and place of reason, that the mind *itself* mattered has

But this is precisely what the Christian mind stands *against*. And
just. Fields of knowledge such as science are *not* totally separated
n spiritual faith. A more honest evaluation was offered by another
ntist, Brian Silver:

cience is not a harmless intellectual pastime. In the last two
enturies we have moved from being simply observers of na-
ure to being, in a modest but growing way, its controller. . . .
cience has to be watched. The layman can no longer afford
o stand to one side, ignorant of the meaning of advances that
ill determine the kind of world that his children will in-
abit—and the kind of children that he will have.[13]

Mark Noll casts the vision for the comprehensive nature of a re-
ed kind of thinking:

y an evangelical "life of the mind" I mean . . . the effort to think
e a Christian—to think within a specifically Christian frame-
ork—across the whole spectrum of modern learning, includ-
g economics and political science, literary criticism and imag-
ative writing, historical inquiry and philosophical studies,
guistics and the history of science, social theory and the arts.[14]

as such a mind ever existed in Christian history? Many times,
lways with significance. Philosopher and theologian Jonathan
ards, educated at Yale and third president of Princeton, was ar-
y the greatest intellect American soil has produced. Beyond his
ering theological genius, he pursued studies in ethics, psychol-
nd metaphysics. He contended that the basic goal of any intel-
s to work toward "the consistency and agreement of our ideas
the ideas of God."[15] This simple premise fueled the develop-
of his mind throughout his life, a mind that many would con-
vas the guiding force behind the First Great Awakening.
ond engaging various fields of thought, it is critical to be able

been without question. Even the early church father Tertullian (c.
160-220), who had little use for philosophy, would have held in dis-
dain any anti-intellectualism that celebrated an undeveloped mind.

Throughout Christian history knowledge has been celebrated for
the key role it plays in spiritual development; knowledge invites contemplation through preparatory reading and Scriptural meditation.[6]
The "two constants of western monastic culture," writes Jean
Leclercq, are "the study of letters" and "the exclusive search for

Personification of the *quadrivium* from ninth-century copy of Boethius's *Arithmetic*

God."[7] The very foundation of the liberal arts as an education can be traced back to the monastic education developed during the Middle Ages. There was sacred learning through the Bible, and secular learning through the seven liberal arts. The *trivium* consisted of grammar, rhetoric and logic; the *quadrivium* surveyed arithmetic, geometry, astronomy and music. The whole of human learning could be gathered into these "arts." But the liberal arts were aimed at something beyond themselves, as evidenced in the very words *trivium* and *quadrivium*—the threefold way and the fourfold way—referring to the way to the wisdom contained in the Word of God.[8] In other words, to the development of a Christian mind.

Mark Noll puts it bluntly: "If evangelicals do not take seriously the larger world of the intellect, we say, in effect, that we want our minds to be shaped by the conventions of our modern universities and the assumptions of Madison Avenue, instead of by God and the servants of God."[9] And even if we do not lose our own minds, we will certainly lose the minds of others. This is the double-edged threat of our day: apart from a Christian mind, we will either be taken captive by the myriad worldviews contending for our attention, or we will fail to make the Christian voice heard above the din. Either we begin to think, or we lose the fight.

THE LOST ART OF THINKING

In a *Books & Culture* interview, Tom Morris conveyed a conversation he had with a woman who invited him on behalf of a local Chamber of Commerce to speak to a group of young leaders on the ethics of decision making. In making her request, she said:

> When I was eighteen and in college, we used to sit up late at night and talk about important things: God, death, good, evil, meaning, love. Now when we get together with friends, all we ever talk about is what the kids are doing, what's on sale at the

mall, and who Notre Dame is playing in footb
Could you come and speak to our group and ma
start talking about the big issues again?[10]

Her sense that she needed to pay attention to the lif
perceptive. We all need to start talking about the
But the call runs deeper—we need to think abou
light of our faith. This is what a Christian mind is
ence between the shallow pools of information an
of wisdom.

However, this is precisely what we tend not to
cumb to a kind of compartmentalization over aga
worldview that addresses the entirety of life. A c
mind is one that separates life into distinct categ
family, HBO, a quiet time, and AOL—*all withou
thinking about one area never informs our think
So one can be a Christian and not reflect—or wors
of reflecting—about science or technology in li
worldview. So issues related to bioethics are seldo
reflection on the nature of humanity and the sar
in light of the Scriptures. Instead, we let CNN tel
tific and technological breakthroughs will mean f
life; we marvel at progress; and then we privately
will be able to afford the procedure. The world
distinct from the world of faith. And those in such
happy to keep it that way.[11] Stephen Jay Gould w

> No scientific theory . . . can pose any threa
> these two great tools of human understanding
> tally separate realms: science as an inquiry
> state of the natural world, religion as a se
> meaning and ethical values.[12]

to think about our faith in relation to *its* significance. In dialogue with the world, the deepest question regarding the Christian faith is "So what?" This simple question gets to the heart of not only thinking Christianly but communicating Christianity itself. Jesus was raised from the dead. *So what?* The Bible is true. *So what?* You can have a personal relationship with God. *So what?* Thomas Oden has observed that the fact of the resurrection may be maintained by Christians, but there is often little interest in our communication of the *significance* of the resurrection.[16] The Christian mind must understand the significance in order to offer it to the world. If we cannot, we will have lost our place in the most critical of conversations—indeed, the only conversation that matters.

This kind of thinking is the essence of what is meant by a Christian *worldview*, a term often used but seldom defined.[17] A worldview is the lens through which we look at the world and therefore think about the world. The apostle Paul told the Ephesians to see with the "eyes of the heart" (Eph 1:8). This is precisely what a worldview involves, for it is based on faith. Brian J. Walsh and J. Richard Middleton suggest that the faith commitment on which our worldview is based can be found in how we answer four questions: (1) *Who am I?* Or what is the nature and purpose of human beings? (2) *Where am I?* Or what is the nature of the universe I live in? (3) *What's wrong?* Or what is the basic problem or obstacle that stands in the way of attaining fulfillment. (4) *What's the remedy?* Or how do we find salvation.[18] Beyond defining the world, a worldview attempts to cast a vision for what the world should be. Without this vision, it is difficult to set a course for others to follow.

THE SOURCE OF THINKING

We see a film and are moved and directed by its sophisticated angles and editing, color and sound. But on what basis do we critique it? Simply by plot or directorial style? I need a mind—a worldview—to

engage what the film's "mind" is saying about truth and relationships, my soul and God. To borrow a simile from Ludwig Wittgenstein, trying to engage the world without a mind shaped to engage
the world is like buying several copies of the same newspaper in order to check whether what the paper said is true.[19]

Having such a uniquely informed mind may be the most dynamic
feature of a Christian's intellect. Secularization has reduced the
foundation of knowledge—at least on the popular level—to that
which can be empirically verified. Yet much that is true does not
come through empirical reasoning but through revelation. It is not
cold, controlled observation alone that is able to produce what can
be known.[20] What decisively marks a Christian mind is that it is informed by revelation (knowledge that unless revealed by God would
not be known) and then proceeds to think in *light* of that revelation.
The foundation of the Christian intellect is its rooting in the Scriptures. Coupled with this is the promptings and leadings, insights and
illuminations that come through the indwelling presence and work
of the Holy Spirit as the mind feeds on God's revealed truths. This
combination of revelation and illumination puts the Christian at a
decided advantage for insight and wisdom.

Contrast this with what feeds most minds in our modern world: information. Not knowledge, wisdom or revelation. Just *information*, virtually unlimited amounts coupled with immediate access. Quentin
Schultze writes that it is little more than "endless volleys of nonsense,
folly and rumor masquerading as knowledge, wisdom, and even
truth."[21] The inadequacy of this cannot be overstated.

One of the most vivid examples of the media's power to set such
an agenda came to me on September 6, 1997, while I was doing my
morning run at the gym. While exercising, I watched the entire
CNN Headline News program from 8:30 to 9 a.m. The first fifteen
minutes was spent on Princess Diana, who had been killed a week
earlier in a car crash. There was a story on her funeral. Then came

a story on her boys and how they would handle her death and the media scrutiny. Then came a report on the song that Elton John had composed for her funeral, followed by footage of the bells pealing throughout England for her death. Next was a story on the eulogies that had been given at her burial. Only two other events, Hurricane Erica and the Space Station Mir, received coverage during the news segment of the program. When these two additional stories were completed, the newscast went back to Elton John singing his new version of *Candle in the Wind*. That was it.

CNN then went right into its business news, its sports segment and then its entertainment coverage. Under normal circumstances, considering this was America's leading cable news network, you would think it was just a slow news day. Or that the death of Princess Diana was such a monumental event that it deserved to dominate the newscast. Yet I knew that something else had happened the night before, something that was never mentioned—*not even once*. There was another death to take note of. A small, old Albanian woman named Agnes had passed away—better known to the world as Mother Teresa. Newsworthy? To say the least. Mother Teresa was a Nobel prize winner and arguably the most beloved woman in the entire world. *She was never even mentioned.*

CNN wasn't alone. According to the Media Research Center, the coverage of Diana to Mother Teresa on the CBS Evening News ran three to one, and on NBC seven to one. *Newsweek* had forty-seven pages on Diana, but only four on Mother Teresa. *Time* and *U.S. News & World Report* weren't much better.[22]

Now we live in a world that allows us to see only what we choose to see, hear only what we choose to hear and read only what we choose to read. Through the technology, we have the ability to filter out everything but what we wish to be exposed to—creating what University of Chicago professor Cass Sunstein has called the "Daily Me," a self-created world in which we see only the sports highlights that concern our favorite team, read only the issues that address our interests and engage only the op-ed pieces we agree with. The highly lauded personalization of information protects us from exposure to anything that might challenge our thinking or make us uncomfortable. Unchecked, we begin to follow the sound of nothing more than the echo of our own voice.[23]

Owen Chadwick insightfully notes that the heart of the problem of the media in a secularized world becomes evident when a fourteen-year-old schoolboy without any personal investigation or reflection declares that "Darwin has disproved the Bible."[24] Why? Because that's what he's "heard." While the media may not tell us what to *think*, it certainly tells us what to think *about*.

DEVELOPING YOUR MIND

To think Christianly, with wisdom and insight, clarity and purpose, demands a Christian mind. But such a mind does not simply appear at conversion. Like our souls, it must be developed. But the development is not dependent on programs or personalities. This is not to discount education—either formal or informal. I am an educator who is deeply committed to the education process. However, borrowing a phrase from Thomas Jefferson, Susan Wise Bauer rightly maintains that any literate man or woman "can rely on self-education to train and fill the mind. All you need are a shelf full of books . . . and a few 'chasms of time not otherwise appropriated.' "[25] It is *reading* followed by *reflection* that drives even the best of educations. Since it begins and then fuels the process, we will spend the most time on reading.

Reading. One of the great gifts my mother gave to me was a love of reading. She could talk about a book as if it was something good to eat. After she described one of the storms Laura faced in *The Long Winter*, an Oompa-Loompa in *Charlie and the Chocolate Factory* or the windswept moors of *Wuthering Heights*, I *had* to read the book. I could actually be disciplined with the threat of "no library for a

week." But reading cannot rest on a mother's gift or a child's procliv-
ity. It must be accepted as an indispensable ingredient in how we are
attempting to develop our lives. "A
monastery without a library," a monk
in Normandy wrote in 1170, "is like a
castle without an armory. Our library
is our armory."[26] St. Cyprian of
Carthage would have agreed, writing,
"Be assiduous in prayer and reading.
In the one you speak to God. In the
other God speaks to you." Even earlier
came the apostle Paul's request from
his prison cell in Rome that Timothy
should bring his books (2 Tim 4:13).

Sir Robert Humphries library,
Bodleian, Oxford

There is no substitute for reading,
and particularly the great books. Robert Maynard Hutchins is correct
in noting that "until lately the West has regarded it as self-evident that
the road to education lay through the great books." What are the great
books? "There never was very much doubt in anybody's mind about
which the masterpieces were," writes Hutchins. "They were the
books that had endured and that the common voice of mankind
called the finest creations, in writing, of the Western mind." Hutchins, along with Mortimer Adler, collected a set that went from Homer
to Freud, over twenty-five centuries, including the works of Plato and
Aristotle, Virgil and Augustine, Shakespeare and Pascal, Locke and
Rousseau, Kant and Hegel, Darwin and Dostoevsky.[27]

Critiques can be made of such reading programs, both in scope
and intent, but at least they propel the reader into what Hutchins
calls the "Great Conversation." Or as Descartes would suggest, the
reading of such books is like a conversation with the noblest men of
past centuries, "nay a carefully studied conversation, in which they
reveal to us none but the best of their thoughts."[28]

So where do we begin? How can we become active readers in the midst of the frantic pace of our lives? It's tempting to view the act of sitting down with a book—much less many books—as a luxury afforded those with unique schedules or privileged positions in life. In truth, it is available to us all.

To read, you must first *position* yourself to read. For my part, I have learned to keep books around me. When I travel, when I take my car to have the oil changed, when I pick my children up from school, I have a book. If you were to look around my house, you would see stacks of books everywhere, on the tables by the side of beds, on the floor by chairs, yes, in almost every bathroom. While the types of books vary greatly, they are not randomly selected. Arthur Schopenhauer said, "If a man wants to read good books, he must make a point of avoiding bad ones; for life is short, and time and energy limited."[29] The great books from the past are easily determined, for we have centuries of evaluation from which to benefit.[30] The best books of our present day are harder to determine, which is why to begin my reading I often turn to book reviews that help sort through the thousands of titles released each year.

But a life of reading is not served solely through the ready access and careful selection of books, but also by knowing the degree to which individual books should be read. Not every book qualifies for a cover-to-cover journey. Long ago, Francis Bacon gave this wise counsel: "Some books are to be tasted, others to be swallowed, and some few to be chewed and digested." In graduate school, my supervisory professor required that each of his doctoral students buy a copy of Mortimer Adler and Charles van Doren's *How to Read a Book*. This may have been the most profitable assignment he gave. As a professor, I often pass the favor on to my students.

Adler offers a commonsense roadmap to the various "levels" of reading in light of what the book deserves. For example, some books need only an inspectional reading. Some might call this skimming, but that gives the impression of it being less of an investment than it really is. It's actually skimming *systematically*. Often there is a good deal that can be learned about a book on the surface, and many books do not require that you go much further. If the most basic level of reading is, What does this sentence say? the question at the inspectional level is, What is this book about? While this is a skill to be developed, the mechanics are simple: (1) look at the title page and its preface, (2) study the table of contents, (3) check the index and (4) read the publisher's blurb. At this point, you will probably know whether the book deserves more than an inspectional reading. Let's assume it doesn't. To complete the inspectional process and finish the book, (5) examine the chapters that seem to be pivotal to the book's argument and (6) finally, turn through the pages, dipping in here and there, reading a paragraph or two, sometimes several pages in sequence but seldom more than that.

If the book *does* warrant more than an inspectional reading, take the work to the next level, which is analytical reading. This is a thorough, complete reading—the best reading that you can accomplish. It is intensely active reading, engaging the text with numerous questions. These books should be "chewed and digested." Adler writes that this level is seldom needed when you are after information; it is to be reserved for the deepest levels of *understanding*. The highest and most complex level of reading would be syntopical, or *comparative* reading. This is when you read many books, seeking to place one book in a larger conversation with others that deal with related issues and ideas. From this you can construct an analysis that may not be in *any* of the books. As a result, I tend to make this investment based not only on the worth of the book but the ideas it engages.

Yet the greatest maneuver to make has nothing at all to do with the mechanics of reading itself. It has to do with the choices we make. I once heard Jim Collins, bestselling author of business titles, comment that we don't need to make more to-do lists but rather a few stop-doing lists. In my life the great opposition to reading is what I allow to fill my time *instead* of reading. And there is little doubt what offers the greatest temptation. By the late 1970s more homes contained a TV than had running water or flush toilets.[31] Former NBC chief Brandon Tartikoff has written that the present generation "has never known a living environment in which there wasn't a television."[32] According to a study reported in the *New York Times*, the average person in America spent about 1,100 hours a year watching broadcast TV, an additional 500 hours watching cable and 300 hours listening to music. Only 100 hours were spent reading.[33] The great fear of George Orwell, as conveyed in his novel *1984*, was of those who would ban books. Aldous Huxley's fear was more prescient; in *Brave New World* he feared there would be no reason to ban a book, for no one would want to read one.[34]

Much of our success with reading will be found in making wise choices and becoming alert to those things that war against sitting down with a book. With the scent of a savvy, real-world reader, Susan Wise Bauer gives the following suggestions that go beyond the first step of turning off the TV: morning is better than evening (why fight the fatigue?), start short (as with physical exercise, work your way into shape, starting with no more than thirty minutes of reading a day), don't schedule yourself for study every day of the week (aim for four days, giving yourself some days off for the inevitable interruptions of life), never check your e-mail right before you start reading (it distracts the mind and commands our time), guard your reading time (set it, keep it, protect it), and take the first step *now*.[35] I will add two more to her list: First, don't attempt to read a book, particularly a significant one, in the context of chaos. Blaring music, kids interrupting you every five minutes, getting up to answer the phone—such distractions are insurmountable. Guarding your reading involves more than setting the time itself aside; it includes protecting the quality of your reading time. Second, do not become discouraged if you read slowly, resulting in only a few books a year. The more you read, the faster you will read. Likewise with comprehension. Your mind is like your body;

you wouldn't expect to run a four-minute mile the first day or complete a marathon after two weeks in the gym. Reading speed and comprehension will come with practice over time.

Prayerful reflection. But reading alone is not enough. In his famed reminder to H. G. Wells, G. K. Chesterton quipped, "The object of opening the mind, as of opening the mouth, is to shut it again on something solid." There is no substitute for prayerful reflection in order to reach some sense of conclusion. Long walks, meditative contemplation—these are the disciplines that forge a mature mind. It has been said that the electronic world has meant a "speeded-up mind," which is precisely what we cannot afford.[36] We must take the time to think carefully and deeply, in conversation and communion with God, and in companionship with the Scriptures. Knowledge, and issues related to knowledge, often take time to settle into our spirits where the Holy Spirit can begin to bring clarity and insight. As Søren Kierkegaard once counseled, "We live forward, but we can only think backward."[37] Apart from this, we are subject to immediate, spontaneous conclusions, which tend to be driven by emotions and expediency.

Reflection is needed to draw not only conclusions from our knowledge but also application. Only through prayerful meditation can we engage the "responsibility" of knowledge.[38] This is the dynamic behind one of the most profound verses in Scripture: "Do not conform any longer to the pattern of this world, but be transformed by the renewing of your mind" (Rom 12:2). The verbs

Auguste Rodin's *The Thinker*

are in the present imperative, which speak to the challenge to continually "go on" refusing to conform to the patterns of the world and
to continually "go on" letting ourselves be renewed by the transforming of our mind. At first glance this seems to mean little more than
morality. Paul is going deeper. Moral choices forge a *character*. The
Phillips paraphrase puts it well: "Don't let the world around you
squeeze you into its own mould." Even better is Eugene Peterson's
The Message: "Don't become so well-adjusted to your culture that
you fit into it without even thinking."

By nature we tend to adapt, to conform, to our surroundings.
There are only two forces shaping us: one is the world and the other
is the will of God. If we are to avoid becoming absorbed in the surrounding culture, we must take a stand. That stand comes through
the renewing of our minds. No wonder we read in the wisdom literature of the Bible that as a man "thinks in his heart, so is he" (Prov
23:7 NKJV). The deepest truths are driven home in my life when I
take them into the sanctuary of God's presence. Alone with him,
apart from the world, the most profound truths take root in my life.
Taken into prayer, ideas become *real*, life-changing, dynamic. Then,
and only then, they change my life.

At the end of his short but profound book *Your Mind Matters*,
John Stott captured these sentiments in the form of a prayer:

> I pray earnestly that God will raise up today a new generation
> of Christian apologists or Christian communicators, who will
> combine an absolute loyalty to the biblical gospel and an un-
> wavering confidence in the power of the Spirit with a deep and
> sensitive understanding of the contemporary alternatives to the
> gospel; who will relate the one to the other with freshness, pun-
> gency, authority and relevance; and who will use their minds
> to reach other minds for Christ.[39]

Few prayers could be more pertinent for our day.

A MOST CONVERTED MIND: THE LIFE OF C. S. LEWIS

On Friday, November 22, 1963, three lives ended within hours of each other. John F. Kennedy, thirty-fifth president of the United States; Aldous Huxley, noted English novelist and critic; and a man known by his friends simply as "Jack." But it was this third and final man that has arguably shaped the most lives.

Clive Staples Lewis was born in Belfast, Ireland. Following World War I (Lewis served in France and was wounded in 1917), he went to University College, Oxford, where he achieved a rare Double First in Classics, an additional First in English and the Chancellor's Prize for academics. He was soon offered a teaching position at Magdalen College, Oxford, where he was a fellow and tutor from 1925-1954, and then later at the University of Cambridge as professor of medieval and Renaissance English (1954-1963).[1]

In 1931 Lewis came out of atheism into the Christian faith, aided significantly through his friendship with J. R. R. Tolkien, author of *The Lord of the Rings*. The intellectual questions that plagued Lewis during his spiritual journey—why God allows pain and suffering, how Christianity can be the one and only way to God, the existence of miracles—became the very questions he helped others navigate as a Christian. Walter Hooper, a longtime friend and personal secretary to Lewis, once commented that Lewis struck him "as the most thoroughly *converted* man" he had ever met.[2]

Lewis produced a torrent of works, eventually reaching forty titles, the vast majority attempting to put forward Christianity in a very non-Christian world. Among the more widely known are a trilogy of science fiction novels (when the genre was hardly known), *The*

Screwtape Letters and the Chronicles of Narnia, a series of seven children's books that are widely heralded as classics of fantasy literature.

Lewis's passion was thoughtfully translating the Christian faith into language that anyone could understand. He was driven to have people know what Christianity was *about.* Through a series of BBC radio addresses during World War II, his conversational style, wit, intellect and rough charm were made known to millions. Lewis was first invited to produce four fifteen-minute talks. The response was so overwhelming that the BBC gave him a fifth fifteen-minute segment to answer listeners' questions. A second round of talks were requested and given. The clarity of thought and his ability to gather together a wide range of information and make it plain led one listener to remark that they "were magnificent, unforgettable. Nobody, before or since, has made such an 'impact' in straight talks of this kind."[3] The BBC asked for a third round of talks, this time stretching out for eight consecutive weeks. Lewis consented but made it clear it would be his last. His goal throughout was simple: "I was . . . writing to expound . . . 'mere' Christianity, which is what it is and was what it was long before I was born."[4] Eventually gathered together in a single work titled *Mere Christianity,* the BBC talks continue to make Christianity known to millions.

ANSWERING THE CALL

*"Vocation or calling is a certain kind of life
ordained and imposed on man by God for the common good."*

WILLIAM PERKINS

"Ask me whether what I have done is my life."

WILLIAM STAFFORD

If you are a Christ follower, you have been deeply and profoundly called by God. And not just once but twice.

You wouldn't be a Christ follower if you hadn't answered the first call. You cannot influence the world around you as fully as God intends without answering the second. God first called your heart to respond to Christ for forgiveness and leadership. The second call on your life, one that is at the center of how Christ wants you to personally penetrate this world and live for him, is the call of vocation.

THE IDEA OF VOCATIO

The word *vocation* comes from the Latin word *vocatio*, which means "summons" or "invitation." The idea is a rich one. Our occupational investments are to be infused with a clear and direct sense of honor and worth as if the task itself was an offering unto God. "Calling is the truth," writes Os Guinness, "that God calls us to himself so decisively that everything we are, everything we do, and everything we have is invested with a special devotion and dynamism lived out as a response to his summons and service."[1]

Perhaps the most overlooked contribution the Reformation made to the modern world is its vigorous pursuit of the recovery of calling, arguing that all of secular life should be made into a vocation of God. Owen Chadwick writes that the Protestant recovery of vocation was like a baptism of the secular world. "It refused any longer to regard the specially religious calling of priest or monk as higher in moral scale than the calling of cobbler or prince."[2] This is the point: once a Christian, your vocational place in life takes on new meaning, and no one's place in life is less of an offering to God than another. The Reformation idea of vocation flows from the monastic vision. Luther, himself a monk, was clearly familiar with the monastic conviction that all tasks needed to be offered as worship of the living God. Each role within the monastic community had intrinsic value and was to be viewed as a gift submitted in devotion. Luther took this fundamental value out of the cloistered confines of the monastic order and applied it to the wider world of the marketplace. But this new "priesthood of all believers" did not make everyone into church workers, reminds Gene Edward Veith. "Rather, it turned every kind of work into a sacred calling."[3]

Medieval monk

As such, the idea of vocation presents a radical break from the privatization of our modern world and a revolutionary expansion of most Christian's thinking about the nature of their lives. Our tendency is to compartmentalize, with our spiritual life over *here* and our jobs over *there*. Yes, we struggle with how to live for Christ in the marketplace in terms of survival and sometimes ethics, but to see the job *itself* as a sacred act of worship is often beyond our spiritual vision. As Henri Nouwen confessed at the beginning of his stay at a Trappist monastery, "Most people think that you go to the monastery to pray. Well, I prayed more this week than before but also discovered that I have not learned yet how to make the work of my hands into a prayer."[4] But this is precisely what the idea of vocation challenges us to pursue.

SOMEONE, NOT SOMETHING

Why is this idea so alien, even to the Christian? Arguably, it is because we not only have tended to privatize our lives, but in the area of vocation we have secularized them. Think of how we use the term itself. We talk of "vocational education" and "vocational counseling," which means little more than job training and job placement. The heart of our calling, however, is not to some*thing* but to *Someone*.[5] The idea behind calling is that whatever our occupation may be, it is to be elevated to an expression of worship—that which could be pleasing to God—if performed with excellence and integrity and heartfelt devotion. A real estate agent, then, as a committed servant is to represent his or her clients to the greater glory of God. A software developer's labor is to be infused with a sense of piety. But this is rare.

"Doctors practice medicine not primarily to relieve suffering, but to make a living," noted Dorothy Sayers. "Lawyers accept briefs not because they have a passion for justice, but because the law is the profession that enables them to live." More often than not, we have reduced being a *Christian* doctor or a *Christian* lawyer to what is done outside of office in some form of "official" ministry setting. The fallacy of this, notes Sayers, is that we view work not as the "expression of man's creative energy in the service of society, but only something he does in order to obtain money and leisure."[6]

It doesn't help that when we first charted our vocational course in life, the notion of calling was seldom used as a compass. For many, the trek began with choosing a major in college. Rather than evaluating gifts and abilities, position or responsibility, submitting the matter to prayer and consideration, we were opportunistically pragmatic. What teachers did we like? Where could we get accepted? Where were the best job opportunities? What would pay the most? This is the map most of us follow our entire life. It's not that we tried to go against the natural grain of our life, much less dismiss the voice of God, we just didn't think of God speaking to us about such things. Yet if the root of *vocation* is "calling," then we must listen. "It means a calling that I hear," writes Parker Palmer. "Before I can tell my life what I want to do with it, I must listen to my life telling me who I am."[7] Or as the Hasidic tale records Rabbi Zusya saying when he was an old man, "In the coming world, they will not ask me: 'Why were you not Moses?' They will ask me: 'Why were you not Zusya?' "[8]

When I became a Christ follower at the age of twenty, I was a premed major in college. I wanted to be a doctor because it paid well and seemed reasonably well-respected. There was no sense whatsoever of it being a life God had called me to pursue. But with my new life in Christ came a new sense of purpose. I wanted nothing more than to live the life that would make the most impact for him. If it was in medicine, fine, but if not, all the better. As I evaluated medicine through the lens of my newfound faith, it became clear that there was little to commend it. I was competent in science but had scant passion for medical matters. And unlike what I had seen God give others who *had* been called to this field, nothing in my spirit sparked a vision for how it could play into the wider scheme of things. But I knew what did. I knew what I could do. *Should* do. Was *made* to do. *Communicate.*

Amazingly, this simple, basic understanding of who I was, and who God had made me to be, had never factored into my thinking about vocation. But all my life I had been a communicator. Whether through music or drama, writing or speaking, teaching or painting,

Calling of St. Matthew by Michelangelo Caravaggio

I was a communicator. There were other dynamics to consider—gifts in leadership, a love of academia and a bent toward analytical thinking—but always with communication as the touchstone. So I changed my major from biology to communications and made plans to develop myself to use whatever abilities God had given me toward building the kingdom. While the specifics are continuing to be worked out decades later, the course itself was set. I had answered God's call for my life.

The most profound vocational question is not What should I do with my life? Instead, it is the more foundational—and demanding—question posed by Parker Palmer: Who am I? "A tree gives glory to God by being a tree," Thomas Merton once wrote.[9] This is true, for God intended the tree to *be* a tree. Yet this is equally true for individuals. If you *are* an artist, you should pursue art. Or as William Romanowski maintains, insofar as Christian artists do *not* create art and music, "that is . . . secularization."[10] You are divorcing God from the natural course of your life in a way that was never intended, for you were made in such a way as to fulfill a specific part of God's design and plan.

Several years ago the film *Chariots of Fire* captured the public's imagination and the year's Oscar for best picture with its story of Eric Liddell, the 1930s Olympic runner from Scotland. In the film Liddell's sister questions him about why he is going to run in the Olympics instead of pursuing another career. In reply, he turns to his sister and says, "Jenny, God made me fast, and when I run, I feel his pleasure." God made each of us a certain way, and when we run that course, we feel pleasure—God's and ours. Frederick Buechner's definition rings true: Vocation is "the place where your deep gladness and the world's deep hunger meet."[11] And make no mistake—the world's deep hunger needs your deep gladness. That's why God gave it to you.

IT'S NOT ABOUT ME

But there is a grave and serious danger when it comes to this aspect of calling. We can reduce God's call on our life to little more than self-indulgence. We can substitute God's grand movement in our life to finding a job that pays us to do what we most enjoy in a setting we find most comfortable. When these factors come together, we think we have found our calling. We talk in terms of pursuing who God made us to be, but it is often a euphemism for personal satisfaction and enjoyment—a kind of spiritualized career assessment that we give ourselves divine license to pursue.

The primary sense of calling is that it is not for *self* but for God's glory. If we are stirred to make a career adjustment, who God made us to be and whatever leadings he provides should certainly be considered, but the higher goal remains doing *whatever* we do, *wherever* we are, with a sense of purpose and meaning. This is the essence of Paul's admonishment to the people at Colosse: "Whatever you do, work at it with all your heart, as working for the Lord, not for men" (Col 3:23). Independent of any individual calling toward a specific area of life, the primary call is to faithfulness to God. Determining whether I am called to be an economist is secondary to the task at hand—if I *am* an economist, I am called to be a *Christian* one who engages work as an act of worship. So vocation is as much about being faithful where we find ourselves as it is finding where we are to be faithful.

Does this mean there is no place for a mid-course correction? Of course not. This is not a passive fatalism that must accept whatever comes our way or a dictate to remain in whatever state we find ourselves. God's leadings are as deep and mysterious as what they reflect, which is nothing less than the moving of the Holy Spirit in our lives. And those are very deep and mysterious movements indeed. But we must guard against the "restlessness," to use Calvin's term, "which prevents an individual from remaining in his condition with a peaceable mind."[12] We can spend our lives trying to find our place only to one day realize our lives have been used up entirely in the search. Our primary call is to look for satisfaction in our work and to discover how to bring honor to God through it. Calling is as much about *how* we are living and for what *purpose* as about what occupation we have. Or as Nouwen once wrote, it is about knowing that "here and now is what counts and is most important because it is God himself who wants me at this time in this place."[13]

This was driven home to me during a time of enormous soul-searching that revolved around turning forty. Like many men, I spent my twenties and thirties in pursuit of goal-oriented accomplishments.

As I approached forty, I knew I was entering a new season of life and
ministry, so I committed myself anew to finding what I was to do with
the rest of my life. Instead of discovery, there was a rude awakening.
As I faced such questions as What do I do best? and Where could I
make the most impact? the unmistakable voice of the Holy Spirit
whispered, "These are the wrong questions." I thought to myself,
*What do you mean these are the wrong questions? They are the ones
everybody else gets to ask!* I didn't want them to be the wrong questions. They were the only questions I knew, and more than that, they
were the ones I most wanted answered. But the troubling idea that I
was misguided did not go away. I began to pray and reflect on what
was wrong with my quest; I searched the Scriptures. All to no avail.

Then my misgivings began to take shape.

It dawned on me that there was not a single case in all of Scripture
where someone went on a journey of self-discovery in order to find
and follow God's vocational call. I could not find a single case in
Scripture where people went on a hunt for their vocational niche in
light of their personality, gifting or experience. I had bought into the
self-absorbed thinking that begins and ends with "who I am in
Christ" (translation: what is my personal makeup and what it would
take to make me fulfilled), and that became a license for the whole-
sale pursuit of personal pleasure.

In my journey through the biblical materials, I found that people
were *invited* to do something (as with Jeremiah or the disciples), *selected* to do something (along the lines of David or Samuel) or presented with the *opportunity* to do something (as were Esther or Deb-
orah). I could not find a single case of someone going off in search
of their innate identity, much less trying to order their steps to fulfill
who they were "made" to be. Not once did a biblical character say,
"This is what would satisfy me, or make me happy, or allow me to be
healthy and whole," and then map out a strategy to make it happen.
They simply lived their life in faithfulness and responded to what

God brought their way. They submitted their gifts and abilities, investments and labor, to him. And even if God never brought anything their way, they embraced their place in life with the belief that at the very least *that* had been brought their way.

This revelation was akin to Thomas Merton's insight that "people who know nothing of God and whose lives are centered on themselves imagine that they can only find themselves by asserting their own desires and ambitions and appetites in a struggle with the rest of the world."[14] I wanted to know what I was to do with the second half of my life, but I was thinking solely in terms of *place* or *situation*—and always in light of *me*. But that was not at the heart of my vocational pursuit. My fundamental calling was not about what I did as much as how I did it. It was not about where I went as much as what I did where I was. If God led beyond that, so be it, but that was not the foremost issue at hand.

God calls us to live large on the very stage we find ourselves. God has placed us in this very situation to infuse it with meaning and significance. This enables us to live for Christ *now* rather than waiting for a set of circumstances we imagine will allow us to serve him in the future. This simple but profound attitude has marked many of the great lives, and not only those in the pages of Scripture. Corrie ten Boom did not seek her place in a German concentration camp, but she responded appropriately, seeing every moment of her life—including those spent under Nazi brutality—as a time of God's call on her life. In like manner, Nelson Mandela did not choose imprisonment on Robbin's Island, but he found his vocation there. Mother Teresa did not envision the slums of Calcutta when entering the ministry as a teenage girl in Albania, but she was committed to the situation God eventually put her in.

This raises perhaps the most powerful but disconcerting dynamic within vocation: accepting a call we do not want—and obeying it no matter what—in humble, faithful submission.

I once ran across an old book that has become a prized part of my library. It is a biography simply titled *Borden of Yale '09*. It tells of a man named William Borden who went to Yale University as an undergraduate and afterward became a missionary candidate to China. Heir to the Borden Dairy estate, he was a millionaire by the time he graduated high school. As a gift on the event of his graduation, Borden was sent on a trip around the world. Traveling throughout Asia, the Middle East and Europe, he experienced a growing concern for the hurting and lost of the world. He wrote home to say, "I'm going to give my life to prepare for the mission field." After making this decision, he wrote two words in the back of his Bible: "No Reserves."

From there Borden went on to Yale University with purpose and determination. During his first semester he began a campuswide student movement to meet regularly, read the Bible and pray. By the end of his first year, 150 fellow freshman were meeting for weekly Bible studies. By the time he was a senior, 1,000 out of Yale's 1,300 students were

William Borden (second from right)

joining together in these groups. Beyond the campus, Borden founded the Yale Hope Mission to reach out to those on the streets of New Haven, Connecticut. All of this was set in the context of his call to foreign missions, which soon focused on Muslims in China. After graduation, Borden was offered numerous high-paying jobs, but he declined them all in order to pursue the mission field. At this point, he wrote down two more words in the back of his Bible: "No Retreats."

Borden next went to graduate school at Princeton Seminary, where he was ordained to the ministry. After he finished his studies, he set sail for China through the China Inland Mission, stopping first in Egypt to study Arabic. While there, he contracted cerebrospinal meningitis. In less than a month, William Borden was dead. He was twenty-six years old. But before his death, knowing that the steps of his life would take him no further, he had written two more words in his Bible; beneath "No Reserves" and "No Retreats" he had written "No Regrets."[15]

This sense of vocation tempers much of the current fascination with "finding your spiritual gift" or "being who you are" as the goal of God's call on our life. Instead, it heightens the relational dimensions of the journey and makes *calling*—in its deepest and most profound sense—the ultimate pursuit. The biblical idea of calling means following wherever God leads. As Walter Brueggemann has observed, this "sense of call in our time is profoundly countercultural," further noting that "the ideology of our time is that we can live 'an uncalled life,' one not referred to any purpose beyond one's self."[16] The tie between vocation and obedience is undeniable. The Latin *vocatio* means a "call." The word *obedience* is derived from the Latin *oboedire*, which shares its roots with *audire*, to hear. "So to obey really means to hear and then act upon what we have heard," offers Esther de Waal, "in other words, to see that the listening achieves its aim."[17] Obedience is the *response* to calling. The voice calls, and we say yes. It is not about our will but his. It is not about personal fulfillment but personal faithfulness. It is not even about our contribution but our *consecration*. It has often been counseled that this is not about gritting our teeth, clenching our fists and saying "I will! I will!" Instead, we are to relax and submit ourselves to God. It is about letting God's life be willed through us.[18]

I find this to be terribly difficult and terrifying in practice. Everything within me wars against another's leadership, even God's. And when I do obey, my obedience is often just that—obedience, not trust; a "have to," not a "want to." Yet in return, even from these meager offerings, the most significant parts of my life are most profoundly fashioned, and I see God's hand most clearly at work. When I reflect on the affect obedience has had on my spiritual life, those times when I simply determine with every fiber of my being to do what I am convinced God wants me to do (regardless of my own desires or consequence), my mind is filled with the image of a master Sculptor chiseling away at a large, unformed piece of granite. With each act of obedience, another chunk of rock falls to the ground, and the figure the Sculptor desires to create comes increasingly into view. But the significance extends further than my life. When I am obedient, it's not simply *my* life being shaped but the lives around me. As I obey, the master Sculptor chisels away at the world as well. No wonder Thomas Kelly reflected, "The times are too tragic, God's sorrow is too great, man's night is too dark, the Cross is too glorious for us to live as we have lived, in anything short of holy obedience."[19]

EVERY CALLING MATTERS

There is a small country town in England I have visited on more than one occasion. From London, it takes at least two trains and a cab to get there. Not exactly on the main tourist path. Yet I find myself drawn time and again to its setting. It is not simply that Haworth (pronounced "Howeth") is lovely—it typifies all an English village should—but that it holds the memory of a family like no other, for in a modest house on the edge of the village lived the Brontës.

Without a doubt the Brontës were the most amazing literary family in recent history. The patriarch, Patrick, had three daughters: Anne, Charlotte and Emily. Patrick was brilliant and gifted, and was an author in his own right, but his daughters took the family's talents to unprecedented heights. Anne wrote *The Tenant of Wildfell Hall*. Charlotte created *Jane Eyre*. Emily penned *Wuthering Heights*. To have one published writer in a family is rare. To have two is virtually unheard of. To have four is without parallel, particularly when so many of their works became classics in English literature.

The Brontës

But there was another member of the family, a brother, Branwell, whom most have never heard of. He was considered the *most* brilliant, the *most* talented, of them all. But also the most tragic.

Though a writer, painter and gifted speaker, he couldn't see himself in such light. He saw little opportunity for his life to take on meaning, much less significance. When he painted himself with three of his siblings, a portrait which hangs to this day in the National Portrait Gallery in London, he went back at a later date and painted over his own face, leaving only his three sisters to be viewed for posterity.

He then drank himself to death.

I have often reflected on the emptiness Branwell must have felt, and his inability to view his life through God's eyes and in light of God's world. His life is not tragic simply because it bore God-given talent and potential but because it *mattered*. All lives do. God desires nothing more than to infuse our hearts and minds with a sense of meaning and purpose, and to call us to the front lines of what he is doing. If there is anything that an understanding of vocation should provide, it is a vision for life itself.

This was the poignant theme in Ernest J. Gaines's novel *A Lesson Before Dying*. Set in a small Cajun Louisiana community in the 1940s, a young black man named Jefferson becomes reluctantly involved in the robbery of a liquor store. The two men with him are killed; so is the owner of the store. Jefferson is accused of murder. At his trial the defense's strategy is to portray the accused as a pitiful example of humanity and intelligence. His lawyer says, "Why, I would just as soon put a hog in the electric chair as this." But Jefferson is condemned to death.

Grant Wiggins, a college-educated black man who returned to Louisiana to teach at the plantation school, finds himself facing a classroom of young Jeffersons every day. He is asked by his aunt, along with the godmother of the condemned Jefferson, to try and reach out to the condemned man in order to grant his life some form of meaning before the execution. The remainder of the book is the journey of both men to prove the lawyer wrong. This is the great lesson before dying—that we are more than just hogs.

But apart from a sense of vocation, this is difficult to grasp, even among the spiritually informed. Henri Nouwen, reflecting on several years worth of work, noted that "it lacked unity. The many things I did during those years seem disjointed, not really relating to each other, not coming from one source." He realized that he had fragmented his life "into many sections that did not really form a unity."[20] But it *was* a unity. He learned that his life, like ours, needed to be *seen* as one and then *lived* as one through pursuit of God's gifting and, supremely, through obedience.

We do not have a "spiritual life"; we have life that is meant to be lived spiritually. Our careers must be approached in light of God's calling and passionately pursued as worship. Beyond this, whatever we find ourselves doing is to be infused with the greatest call of all:

faithfulness. Without this deep and profound sense of vocation, we will simply race through schedules, build portfolios, climb corporate ladders and optimize our retirement plans for little more than economic benefit. Worse, we will fail to fulfill God's plan for our lives as marketplace men and women. We need those who *are* artists to *be* artists, thinking and acting Christianly *as* artists. The same is true of those in sales, marketing, engineering, teaching and real estate. Christians fueled by a profound sense of calling will revolutionize and reform the fabric of daily life and radically challenge those lives they interact with. Further, when we find ourselves in places not of our choosing or desire, we will rise to the occasion and allow God to influence everyone around us. When we accept our calling and offer it to God in worship and obedience, it becomes a conduit for God's glory and work on this planet.[21]

SOMETHING BEAUTIFUL
FOR GOD:
THE LIFE OF MOTHER TERESA

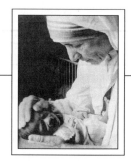

At the tender age of eighteen, the daughter of an Albanian grocer felt a call on
her life to become a nun.[1] Young Agnes
went to Ireland to join the Sisters of Lor-
etto at the Institute of the Blessed Virgin Mary, but six weeks later
she was asked to sail to India as a teacher, where she taught for the
next seventeen years. There she found a "call within a call" to devote
herself to the poor, sick and dying in the slums of Calcutta, eventually living in the slums herself to meet them at their point of need.

Thinking her obedience meant little beyond the lives of those
she served by herself, she was surprised to find those sympathetic to
her efforts soon flocking to her side. Dispensaries and schools were
organized. In 1950 her order received canonical sanction from Pope
Pius XII, and in 1965 it became a pontifical congregation (subject
only to the pope). Under her guidance the order opened centers
serving the blind, the elderly, lepers and the disabled. In 1979 she
was awarded the Nobel Peace Prize for her humanitarian work
around the world. At the time of her death the Order of the Mission-
aries of Charity included hundreds of centers in more than ninety
countries with over four thousand nuns along with hundreds of
thousands of lay workers. Within two years of her death, the process
to declare her a saint had begun.

Few personalities have engaged the world as has Mother Teresa of
Calcutta (1910-1997). "The definition of Mother Teresa is at once
very simple and very complex," reflects David Aikman, a former cor-
respondent for *Time* magazine. It was her conviction that all men
and women of God were called. In talking to him about her voca-

tion, she turned the conversation around and addressed his profession of journalism: "Your work is different. Your task is to do as good a job writing as you can. This is how you may glorify God, by writing the truth and not expressing a bad influence." She then added as if in conclusion, "We express our adoration of God in our work."[2]

For any vocation to be fulfilling, it must not only be heard as a call, it must be responded to through obedience. Little wonder that those closest to Mother Teresa were impressed not simply with her ministry but that anyone would ever have entered into it. "To choose, as Mother Teresa did, to live in the slums of Calcutta, amidst all the dirt and disease and misery," Malcolm Muggeridge once wrote, "signified a spirit so indomitable, a faith so intractable, a love so abounding, that I felt abashed."[3] For Mother Teresa, all of life was to be lived as an obedient answer to God's call. She once described herself as being "God's pencil. A tiny bit of pencil with which he writes what he likes."[4] In concluding his work, Muggeridge reflects that it would be for posterity to decide whether she is a saint. "I only say of her that in a dark time she is a burning and shining light; in a cruel time, a living embodiment of Christ's gospel of love; in a godless time, the Word dwelling among us, full of grace and truth."[5] She simply said, "if [God] gives vocations it's a sign that he wants us to go."[6] And, I might add, to then act.

ALIGNING WITH
THE CHURCH

"I will build my church."

JESUS

"Work hard, then, on the disappointment or anticlimax
which is certainly coming to the patient during his
first few weeks as a churchman."

SCREWTAPE, *THE SCREWTAPE LETTERS*

There is something more profound than a developed soul. There is something more influential than a Christian mind. There is something more compelling than a call. This great enterprise gathers these elements together and places them in a context of such cosmic significance that Jesus declared it would be "so expansive with energy that not even the gates of hell will be able to keep it out" (Mt 16:18 *The Message*).

He was referring to the church.

Jesus made this staggering claim because the church would be his ongoing incarnation on planet earth. The church is his body, his presence, his life—the means for his ongoing ministry to the world, not simply as the universal body of believers around the world but as concrete communities of faith gathered together in the name of Christ as mission outposts to the world. And you cannot fulfill God's plan for your life, much less change the world, apart from taking your place in its mission and ministry, community and cause.

Reflecting on a lifetime of study in the social sciences, Peter Berger suggests that the key to resisting the secular culture of our day is for communities of faith to self-consciously and determinedly stand against the secular onslaught.[1] As critical as it is to understand the process of secularization, it pales in comparison to grasping the church's mandate to engage in "countersecularization." The church, writes Dennis Hollinger, is the "visible, corporate expression of the Christian worldview."[2] Famed missiologist Lesslie Newbigin would agree: "I have come to feel that the primary reality of which we have to take account in seeking for a Christian impact on public life is the Christian congregation. . . . Jesus . . . did not write a book but formed a community."[3]

During World War II the people of London were subjected to the fierce blitzkrieg attacks of the German air force. Throughout the

St. Paul's Cathedral standing proud

blitz St. Paul's Cathedral miraculously escaped major bomb damage, though surrounding areas were reduced to rubble. Rising strong and tall against the London skyline, St. Paul's became the symbol of London's soul, and its spirit was the foundation on which the city would be rebuilt. Like St. Paul's, the church alone can withstand the onslaught of the world and, standing firm, recapture the soul of a lost and weary world.

This is our mission—indeed, our great commission: through the church we are to reach out to those relationally divorced from Christ and turn them into fully-devoted followers (see Mt 28:18-20). No other endeavor could eclipse the global impact of this cause.

But it won't just happen.

We do not live and breathe in a neutral environment but in the midst of a hostile conflict, and we are behind enemy lines. The god of this world has been named, and he is ensconced firmly on his throne. There is only one domain beyond his control that stands in the way of total dominion: the body of Christ. As a result, the church is under constant assault, for it stands alone against the night. It demands constant reinforcement and steadfast commitment. The church is not simply in the vanguard of kingdom advance, it is the entire assault force. According to Jesus' words, the church is not only to take a stand against evil but also to stage a frontal attack.

RESTORING THE CHURCH

Tragically, Christ followers are notorious for being dismissive of the church, as if it were a disposable institution created by human beings as one option on the Christian front, not realizing it is the front *itself*. This is particularly true among evangelical Christians.

Carl F. H. Henry, the founding editor of *Christianity Today* magazine, wrote a masterful six-volume systematic theology that set the stage for evangelical thinking for his generation. *God, Revelation and Authority* insightfully explores the nature of theology and theological method; revelation, inspiration and the canon of Scripture; and the existence and attributes of God, including the Trinity. It pursues issues related to creation and providence, human nature, and original and actual sin. It moves on to investigate the person and work of Christ, predestination, conversion, justification, sanctification, the work of the Holy Spirit, perseverance and, in the end, eschatology. Every major doctrine is covered, save one.

The *church*.

The apparent summa of evangelical thought, and not a single section on ecclesiology. This is nothing against Carl Henry. As a graduate student, I found him to be a gracious and generous man. But he

didn't seem to have a vision for the church. Few American evangelicals have, not simply because our theologians have not led us but
because our enterprising spirit has numbed us to the *primacy* of the
church—particularly through the explosion of the parachurch
movement, aptly described as "religion gone entrepreneurial."⁴ Missions and ministries, crusades and campaigns litter the American religious landscape, most without direct ties to the local church. Embraced as a way to enlarge the boundaries of God's work beyond the
traditional church, for many, parachurch organizations have become a substitute entity, often competing with and occasionally an-
tagonistic toward the church. Almost half of all religious giving now
goes to such enterprises.

To celebrate this trend from being church-centered to kingdom-
centered is terrible theology. The church *is* the divinely instituted
and appointed vehicle of kingdom ministry. The very meaning of
the word *parachurch* is "that which comes along beside [*para*] the
church." It does not mean "beyond the church," as some have suggested. Misunderstanding the nature and role of the parachurch
has led some to actually speak of the "potential" partnership of the
church and parachurch, as if it might be a nice option.⁵ This devaluation of the church in terms of theology, attitude, commitment
and participation is a startling compromise of Christ's vision and intent. The church is not optional for the Christ follower. There is no
ministry found in the New Testament that is not firmly planted under its canopy.

But the critical importance of the church goes well beyond strategic primacy. The church is decisive for the Christian to fulfill the
Christian *life*. Consider what has been entrusted to the church for
the sake of the Christian: the very proclamation of the gospel, corporate worship, the sacraments, the new community in Christ, the use
of and benefit from spiritual gifts, spiritual care and protection
through pastors. Far beyond the church's role as the means by which

the world is to be engaged and transformed, the church is the very body of Christ, which every Christ follower is an integral part of and is meant to embrace (1 Cor 12:12-26). So penetrating was this understanding at the beginning of the Christian movement that it led the early church father Tertullian to maintain "it is not possible to have God as Father without having the Church as mother." Cyprian echoed this sentiment with the dictum, *"Nulla salus extra ecclesiam"*— "outside of the church, there is no salvation."

RETHINKING THE CHURCH

But what about the church's ability to *be* the church? Many have devalued the church and operated outside of its structures because the church has failed to fulfill its mandate in terms of orthodoxy, practice and, most often, mission. When I first became a Christ follower, giving my life to the church was the last thing I would have dreamed of doing. When I looked at the church, all I saw—or thought I saw— was a dead, stagnant, graying organization that was as far from the cutting edge of making a difference in this world as I could imagine. And in truth, many local churches were.

The church must not only be restored to its rightful place in our thought and lives but rethought in terms of mission effectiveness. Doing this will demand scrutinizing tired methods, inane traditions and outmoded approaches to outreach. Unfortunately, even broaching this subject is confusing to many Christians. Those who write the most about addressing our culture tend to set up contemporary approaches to ministry as their favorite straw man to knock down (as if the church's methodology is behind cultural compromise). To some, the real culture war is not between a Christian worldview and secularization but between organs and drums, liturgy and Power-Point. This reveals a tragic inability to see the heart of the issue, which effectively marginalizes the church. As things now stand, many Christians never darken the church's doorway (or take its efforts seriously) because of tired, dilapidated wineskins. Those who attempt to return to a cutting edge ministry on the frontline of king dom advance are denounced as selling out to culture. This stale-mate must be breached.

Lesslie Newbigin reminds us that "the gospel is addressed to hu-man beings. . . . If the gospel is to be understood . . . it has to be com-municated in the language of those to whom it is addressed and has to be clothed in symbols which are meaningful to them."[6] He is not advocating an uncritical pursuit of relevance devoid of faithfulness, or redefining ourselves in ways that are compelling to the world but alien to Christ. We need to clearly distinguish between tradition and traditionalism. Tradition is a good thing. Traditionalism is not. One of the great dangers we face is when individuals build theological fences around their personal tastes and then decry everything out-side of their subjective boundaries as unorthodox. There are lofty ar-guments regarding form shaping content, but this is often disingen-uous. Richard Mouw has reflected on those inclined to denounce newer methods and styles out of hand: "Some of these scholars, I sus-pect, simply do not like popular evangelicalism very much."[7]

Historian Nathan Hatch has noted that it is the *embrace* of new approaches to worship, ministry, evangelism and even organization that have historically fueled the Christian movement, particularly in the North American context. Hatch contends that it was the *popular* religious movements in the half century after American indepen-dence that did more to Christianize American society than anything before or since. Most to the point, Hatch observes that religious lead-ers "went outside normal . . . frameworks to develop large followings by the democratic art of persuasion. . . . They were alike in their abil-ity to portray, in compelling terms, the deepest hopes and aspirations of popular constituencies."[8]

Consider the camp meeting, championed by Francis Asbury but initially met with great skepticism by Methodist authorities. They

Camp meeting

perceived "a manifest subversiveness in the form and structure of the camp meeting itself, which openly defied ecclesiastical standards of time, space, authority and liturgical form." Camp meetings encouraged "uncensored testimonials . . . the public sharing of private ecstasy; overt physical display and emotional release; loud and spontaneous response to preaching; and the use of folk music that would have chilled the marrow of Charles Wesley."[9] Yet the camp meetings brought together three to four million Americans annually, an estimated one-third of the total population of the time. It was a phenomenally successful instrument for popular recruitment, and without question it was used greatly by God. Asbury simply referred to them as "fishing with a large net." This "audience centered" approach, writes Hatch, "meant that the church prospered."[10]

The dynamic of many great movements of God has been the embrace of unconventional methods that connected with the audience in order to present Christ. Consider Luther's move away from Latin when attempting to convey the Scriptures to the German people.

He knew that he could be far more effective and establish rapport with the peasantry far more compellingly if he preached in and had the Bible translated into the German language. William Tyndale, in another context and with another language, did the same a generation before. Or think of Dwight Moody, who preached in theaters and circuses, and used songs written by Ira Sankey that echoed the popular styles of the day (the waltz). During his famous World's Fair campaign of 1893 in Chicago, shortly before his death, Moody even advertised his ministry in the amusement columns of newspapers.[11]

Every generation must translate the gospel into its unique cultural context. This is very different from transforming the message of the gospel into something that was never intended by the biblical witness. *Transformation* of the message must be avoided at all costs. *Translation*, however, is essential for a winsome and compelling presentation of the gospel of Christ.[12] Charles Colson wisely writes that "many churches . . . have found the right balance; behind all the music and skits and fanfare stands a solidly orthodox message that

Urbana worship team

deepens the spiritual life of the members. This is the key. What matters is not whether a church uses skits or contemporary music or squash courts. What matters is biblical fidelity."[13]

BECOMING A MEMBER

So we should not dismiss the church on any pretense but rather embrace the church, bringing our soul, our mind and our sense of calling into what Christ established as the vehicle for world change. This begins by taking our place in the church as a *member*. While there are many forms of church polity, most Christians agree that you must belong to a local church, for unless you do, you cannot align yourself fully with its community. One of the more unsettling revelations to most Christ followers, particularly in light of our fierce individualism, is how many of the marks of a Christian involve other people. You cannot truly follow Christ apart from community, for so much of what is involved in following him is tied to the "one anothers" of Scripture. Originally sent as apostolic admonishments to Christians gathered in local churches, they include such directives as "serve one another" (Gal 5:13), "encourage one another" (1 Thess 5:11), "accept one another" (Rom 15:7) and "bear with . . . and forgive . . . one another" (Col 3:13). These are clear in their command, decisive in spiritual formation and impossible to fulfill apart from a local community of faith. That is their design—they are expressly directed to local church communities and are intended to find their fulfillment within the church family. Jesus maintained that the practice of such community, brought to life in and through the church, would offer the ultimate witness to the world about his own life and ministry (Jn 13:34-35; 17:20-24). Jesus was convinced that the church, functioning as a community of love and witness, would arrest the attention of the world and give ultimate affirmation to his message of salvation. If we fail to participate in this community, we undermine how Christ envisioned his message being affirmed in the eyes of the world.

BECOMING A WORSHIPER

The church is not merely a community; it is a *worshiping* commu
nity. The word *worship* comes from an old Anglo-Saxon word that literally reads "worth-ship," indicating the giving of honor or worth to
someone or something. It is through the church that we ascribe
worth to God. But we also *receive*.

Theologian Geoffrey Wainwright maintains that through the
worship of the church "a vision of reality which helps decisively in
the interpretation of life and the world" is transmitted. Going further, Wainwright contends that the church takes the vision of the
theologian and makes it known; thus "worship is the place in which
that vision comes to a sharp focus."[14] The celebration of the church
is worship, and through worship we not only gain a vision of God but
are transformed by it. The importance of this is found in the ancient
Latin tag *lex orandi, lex credendi* ("the law of praying, the law of believing"). What is prayed indicates what may and must be believed.
Participating in the worshiping life of the church is what best enables us to order our lives around God. Richard Foster notes, "If worship does not change us, it has not been worship."[15] Corporate worship helps us encounter and experience God in a way unlike any
other. Jesus promised, "where two or three come together in my
name, there am I with them" (Mt 18:20). What could be more transforming—both personally and throughout our world—than to have
the very presence of Christ in our midst? This is the promise and reality of worship in the life of the church.

BECOMING A MINISTER

I am often staggered at the lack of vision Christ followers have in regard to the ministry potential of the church. But it is not their fault—
no one is casting a vision before them.

Some of the most successful marketplace leaders in our community—CEOs and lawyers, entrepreneurs and bankers—spent a one-day retreat with the leaders of our church's management team in order to give them a vision of how their lives could be invested in the cause of Christ through the church. It said volumes about them that they would set aside an entire day to gain a spiritual vista in the middle of the week. They even turned off their cell phones.

As we talked about opportunities involving AIDS orphans in Africa, coming alongside churches in Sweden, developing the ministry potential of our church campus and taking advantage of recent technology to establish satellite campuses to expand our outreach to the unchurched of our city, I saw men and women who had never dreamed that they could give their life to such adventures—much less that the church would be the conduit. They experienced the adrenaline rush of being on the front lines for Christ and the expansion of his kingdom. As one said to me afterward, "Mergers and acquisitions don't seem quite as exciting to me right now."

Few Christians see themselves as active ministers in the life of the church. Participants, supporters and donors perhaps, but *ministers?* That is for the select few who receive a unique calling from God. This is one of the most tragic misunderstandings invading Christianity today. *Every* member of a church is a minister, personally gifted and called by God. The apostle Paul wrote that the church is a *body* made up of many parts—legs and arms, eyes and ears, hands and nose. The analogy was not simply a reference to the varying backgrounds, experiences, personalities and ethnicities we bring. Paul was referring to the wonder and might of the Holy Spirit's myriad gifts to believers for the supernatural operation of the church's ministry and pursuit of the church's mission. For Paul, these gifts are real, and our responsibility to them is clear:

> And now, . . . I will write about the special abilities the Holy
> Spirit gives to each of us, . . . there are different kinds of spiri-

tual gifts, but it is the same Holy Spirit who is the source of them all. There are different kinds of service in the church, but it is the same Lord we are serving. There are different ways God works in our lives, but it is the same God who does the work through all of us. A spiritual gift is given to each of us as a means of helping the entire church. (1 Cor 12:1, 4-7 NLT)

At the church I serve, a home-schooling mother of four uses her teaching gifts to be one of our Institute instructors, a bank executive with gifts of administration and mercy oversees our initiative with AIDS orphans in Africa, organizational leadership ability enables the head of our city's ambulance system to spearhead our campus satellite expansions. The gifts of serving and helps coupled with a passion for children leads a young business entrepreneur to sprawl out on the floor with four-year-olds every weekend. Together, these Christ followers enable our church to impact our city and world.

BECOMING A MISSIONARY

Yet the ministry of the church having the greatest effect on our world is missions, with each member serving as a missionary.

By the end of the fourth century, as Christianity became established as the official religion of the empire, it spread first to those in the cities. Those who lived outside of the major cities were among those last exposed to the Christian faith and, consequently, clung the longest to the older ways. Hence the word *pagan*, which originally meant "country-dweller." But these were not militant refusers of the faith. These people were "pagans" because Christianity had not *come* to them. Christianity had been declared the official religion of the empire, but it had not been carried forth to all who might hear. They were "pagan" because of the inadequacy of the church's missionary effort.[16]

The church is called to be an evangelistic enterprise, and its members are to be evangelists. The apostle Paul declared, "We are therefore Christ's ambassadors, as though God were making his appeal through us" (2 Cor 5:20). Typical nonbelievers do not have close relationships with Christ followers. They tend not to watch Christian television or listen to Christian radio. Most are effectively insulated from the Christian message. The only way that they will be reached is through *relationships.* In the context of such relationships the Christian's deepened soul, developed mind and answered call affect the lives of the unchurched, and ultimately bring them into the new community. The hope of the world rests on the mission of the church; the mission of the church rests on individuals infusing their life with evangelistic intent. Lee Strobel, a former atheist turned Christ follower, reminds his new brothers and sisters in the faith that the unchurched need people to strategically venture into their environment to build relational bridges through which the gospel can be communicated.[17] This is how the early church was built, life by life, believers reaching out to those on the fringes of faith. Michael Green, in his study of the sociology of the early church, came to the conclusion that the heart of the early church's growth was simple: they shared the good news of God like it was gossip over the backyard fence.[18]

A FINAL WORD

The church that Christ envisioned and commissioned is to be on the front lines of the battle, reaching deep into the heart of enemy territory. Hell cannot mount a defense against the onslaught of the church. In his book *Courageous Leadership,* Bill Hybels talks about having a defining moment on the place of church in his life.[19] It was the mid-1980s. He'd been out of the country for several weeks on a speaking trip and was returning to the United States through San Juan, Puerto Rico. He'd been outside of CNN range for most of the trip, so he was eager to grab a copy of USA *Today* to catch up.

Then it began

Two young boys—looking to be brothers—started squabbling with each other. The older kid appeared to be seven or eight, the younger around five. Bill watched them a few seconds over the top of his paper, kind of irritated at how they were disturbing him and everyone else.

But he thought to himself, *Boys will be boys.*

Then he heard it: Whack!

He put down his paper because it was obvious that the older boy had just slapped his younger brother—*hard*—right across the face. The smaller boy was crying, and you could already see a nasty welt rising on his cheek. Bill looked around for a parent or anybody responsible for these kids who could stop the mayhem. Then the entire gate area was silenced by a sound that none of them would forget for a long, long time: a closed fist smashing into a face. While the little boy was still crying from the first slap, the older boy had wound up and belted him again, literally knocking the little guy off his feet.

That was more than Bill could take. He blurted out, "Where are these kids' parents?"

No response.

As he raced over to the boys, the older boy grabbed the little guy by the hair and started pounding his face into the tile floor. Bam! Bam! Bam!

Bill then heard the final boarding call for his flight, but he was too sickened by the fight to abandon his mission. He grabbed the older boy by the arm and hauled him off the younger one; then he held them as far apart as he could. With one arm extending out to a kid with a bloody face, and the other straining to stop a boy with murder in his eyes, he knew he was holding a human tragedy in his hands. Just then the ticket agent came up and said, "If you're Mr. Hybels, you've got to board this plane immediately. It's leaving now!" Reluctantly, he loosed his hold on the boys, gathered his things, and rushed backwards down the gangplank, shouting out to the ticket agent, "Keep those kids apart! Please! And find their parents!"

He stumbled on to the plane and managed to find his seat, but he was badly shaken by what had happened. He couldn't get the sights and sounds of the violence he had witnessed between those two young boys out of his head. He grabbed a magazine and tried to read but couldn't concentrate. Then he looked in the entertainment magazine to see what movie would be shown, hoping it would be something that would distract his thinking. But then he sensed the Holy Spirit telling him not to purge his mind so quickly. He sensed a prompting: "Think about what you saw. Consider the implications. Let your heart be gripped by this reality." So he did.

He began to dwell on what he'd seen, and his mind became flooded with thoughts about the older boy's life. He wondered where his parents were. He wondered what kind of experience he was having in school. He wondered if there was anybody in his life offering him love and guidance and hope. He wondered what his future held. If he's throwing fists at the age of eight, what will he be throwing at eighteen? Knives? Bullets?

Where will he end up?

In a nice house with a good wife and a satisfying job? Or in a jail cell, or an early grave?

Then Bill felt prompted to consider what might change the trajectory of that kid's life. He mentally scrolled through the op-

Juvenile under arrest

tions. Maybe, he thought, if we elect some really great government officials who will pass new legislation, maybe that would help a kid like this.

But will it? No doubt, what governments do is very important. Writing legislation for the good of a society is a noble and worthy task. But politicians, no matter how sincere their motivation, can only do so much. They can rearrange the yard markers on the playing field of life, but they can't change a human heart. They can't heal a wounded soul. They can't turn hatred into love. They can't bring about repentance, forgiveness, reconciliation or peace. They can't get to the core problem of the kid he saw in the airport and the millions of others like him.

Bill began to scroll through every option he could think of. *Businessmen* can provide sorely needed jobs. Wise *educators* can teach useful knowledge of the world. *Self-help programs* can offer some occasional methods of behavior modification. *Advanced psychological techniques* can aid self-understanding. And all of that is good—but can any of it truly transform the human heart? No.

Then it came to him like never before. There is only one power that exists on this planet that can change a heart. It's the power of the love of Jesus Christ, the love that conquers sin and wipes out shame and heals wounds and reconciles enemies and patches broken dreams and ultimately changes the world, one life at a time. And the radical message of that transforming love has been given to the church, which is why the church is the most beautiful, the most radical, the most dangerous, the most glorious enterprise on the planet. There is nothing more worthy of our lives investment.

This is how Bill gathered his final thoughts:

There is nothing like the local church when it's working right. Its beauty is indescribable. Its power is breathtaking. Its potential is unlimited. It comforts the grieving and heals the broken in the context of community. It builds bridges to seekers and offers truth to the confused. It provides resources for those in need and opens its arms to the forgotten, the downtrodden, the disillusioned. It breaks the chains of addictions, frees the oppressed, and offers belonging to the marginalized of this world. Whatever the capacity for human suffering, the church has a greater capacity for healing and wholeness.[20]

This is what we have been called to give our lives to, and in order to change the world, what we *must* give our lives to.

THE WILD BOAR
IN THE VINEYARD:
THE LIFE OF MARTIN LUTHER

Martin Luther was born in Saxony in
1483. Schooled in Erfurt, he later fled to
an Augustinian monastery. Literally.
Caught in a thunderstorm, in terror be-
fore the lightning, he cried out, "Help, St. Anne, I will become a
monk!" Despite this less than auspicious beginning, from that point
on Martin Luther was a man of the church. So much so that his passion *for* the church would spark one of the most defining moments
in the history of the church, the Protestant Reformation.[1]

The Reformation was more than theological; it was *ecclesiastical*.
It was a reformation of the *church*. Even the famed ninety-five theses
nailed onto the Wittenberg door say nothing about justification by
faith, the authority of the Bible, the priesthood of all believers or any
of the other well-known Reformation doctrines. Instead, they look
like a treatise on church practice.[2] Luther's ultimate vision for reformation was for a church where each member could play an active
and decisive part, the distinction between clergy and laity could be
dissolved and every believer be seen as a priest, and thus be able to
powerfully "espouse the cause of the faith" to a lost and dying world.[3]

As a result Luther encouraged his fellow monks to break out of the
monasteries and walk among those in the world. He encouraged
those in the world to see their place in life as deeply "called" as those
of the monks, and to take their place in the church's enterprise as fellow ministers. Luther translated Scripture into the native language
of the German people so that they could read, hear and understand
its plain meaning. "You have to ask the housewife, the children in
the street and the ordinary man at the market, see how they respond,

and then translate accordingly," Luther maintained.[4] He believed that preaching should be crafted with the simple and the uneducated in mind. His working motto was keep it simple for the simple.[5] He restored congregational singing; at the time, only priests and monastic choirs would sing during worship, in Latin. Luther wrote hymns that the people would actually enjoy and invited all to sing, such as "A Mighty Fortress Is Our God," crafting tunes that had much in common with what would have been heard in the taverns.[6]

In taking the measure of Luther, historian Roland Bainton sees Luther's greatest contribution to be in the renewal of the mission of the church.[7] Luther not only opened the doors of the church for those to whom it had been closed but cast a vision for how a life investment in the church could make a difference in the world. Not all assessed Luther's efforts in glowing terms. One treatise written against Luther during his own day and presented to the pope opened with the words "A wild boar has invaded thy vineyard." Perhaps. But by the time the boar had finished his tear through the field, a new wine had been cultivated, giving rise to a new wineskin that would spread renewal throughout Christendom.

CONCLUSION

In his grand travel narrative throughout the United States, Robert D. Kaplan captures the reflections of a Navajo Indian who works as a local cable TV employee:

Look all around you in the Southwest; most of the buildings you see are mobile homes. Inside most of these homes are filthy people who can't read, who don't talk to each other, who have few or no relatives or friends, who are one unpaid bill or one small tragedy away from being homeless; people who can't put food on the table or watch over their kids. The little money they have is used to install cable TV. I know. I go into these places every day. . . . When I think of the future of the United States, I think of a little girl I saw inside one mobile home, a girl who—I can tell you from my own experience—is not so untypical. She's about three years old. Her parents plop her down all day by the TV, turned to the channel for soap operas and game shows. There's dirt all over the house. There are tabloid magazines and TV schedules and beer cans. There's not much furniture, no books. It smells.

Reflecting on his own words, the man continues:

> But then, time and again, I will install a cable TV line in one
> of those homes . . . of the rich people, where they put plastic
> on the carpet for me to walk on, so my work boots won't dirty
> the carpet. In rich people's homes it doesn't smell and there
> are always at least a few books, sometimes a lot. That's culture,
> not money.
>
> And there's nothing much in between—between the homes
> with the plastic for me to walk on and those with a trail of gar-
> bage leading from the TV.[1]

His conclusion? "Our culture . . . is getting real thin."

It would be understandable to see this as a reflection of the dispar-
ity between the rich and the poor, but the man was right—it is less
about money than it is *culture*. As such, it also strikes me as a metaphor for the growing chasm between the lives of those formed by the
world and those who are being formed by Christ, and of the cultures
these two tend to create. There is not much in between, and the reason is because our culture is getting thin, stripped of spiritual depth
and weight.

THE BYSTANDER PROBLEM

In the ancient world the influence of Christians acting as salt and
light brought a stop to infanticide, ended slavery, liberated women
and created hospitals, orphanages and schools. During the medieval
era, Christianity kept classical culture alive through copying manu-
scripts, building libraries and inventing colleges and universities. In
the modern era, Christians led the way in the development of science, political and economic freedom, and provided what is arguably the greatest source of inspiration for art, literature and music.[2]
What will Christians do in our day?

The great danger is *nothing*.

One of the most tragic events in recent American history occurred in New York City in 1964. A young woman from Queens named Kitty Genovese was stabbed to death. Over the course of thirty minutes she was chased by an assailant and attacked three times on the street. Thirty-eight of her neighbors watched from their windows. During the entire ordeal not a single person came to her aid. Not a single person shouted out or called for help. No one came to her rescue. No one even bothered to pick up a phone to call the police.

They simply watched.

In a book written after the infamous assault, Abe Rosenthal—who would later become editor of the *New York Times*—offered an explanation for why something like that could happen. For a long time, what he said made intuitive sense to many people and helped them explain it all away. He contended that "Nobody can say [for sure] why the thirty-eight did not lift the phone while Miss Genovese was being attacked . . . [but] it can be assumed . . . that their apathy was . . . almost [certainly] a matter of psychological survival." What Rosenthal meant is that in a world where you are surrounded by millions of people, with millions of needs and issues and urgencies and cries for help, the only way you can survive is to become, as the musical group Pink Floyd would later suggest, "comfortably numb." Rosenthal went on

Kitty Genovese

to say that this "indifference" can become a "conditioned reflex."[3]

Two New York City psychologists—one from Columbia University, the other from New York University—decided that they wanted to dig deeper into what they called the "bystander problem." In a fascinating set of studies, these two psychologists decided that they would stage a series of emergencies of differing kinds and in different settings in order to see who would help. They discovered that there was one single factor that determined whether or not people would respond to a need. It wasn't the severity of the crisis or the degree to which the person screamed or called for help; it wasn't the character of the people in the experiment, whether they were young or old, male or female, black or white. What mattered was how many witnesses there were to the event. The more people who were around, the less people tended to respond.

In one of the experiments the researchers had a student—by himself in a room—stage an epileptic fit. When there was just one person next door listening, that person rushed to the student's aid 85 percent of the time. But when subjects thought that there were as few as four others who also overheard the person having the seizure, they responded only 31 percent of the time. In another staged setting, people who saw smoke seeping out from under a doorway would report it 75 percent of the time when they were on their own, but the incident would be reported only 38 percent of the time when they were in a group.

From these and other tests they discovered that when people are in a group, responsibility for taking personal action becomes diffused. People assume that someone else will make the call, report the problem or respond to the need. Or they assume that because no one else is acting, the apparent problem—whether it is the sounds of someone having a seizure or smoke coming out from under a door—isn't really a problem. If it were, someone would be doing something. Since no one else is responding, there must not be a problem. Because others are around—witnessing what they are witnessing, experiencing what they are experiencing—the sense of personal duty and responsibility is somehow lessened. So in the case of Kitty Genovese, social psychologists argue that the lesson isn't that no one called *despite* the fact that thirty-eight people heard her scream; no one called *because* thirty-eight people heard her scream. If she had been attacked on a lonely street with just one witness, she might have lived: there would have been a sense of *personal* obligation. The sole witness would have been motivated by the fact that it really was up to him or her.[4]

The danger of our day is the absence of a sense of personal responsibility. Our temptation is to assume that things do not depend on us. The idea that what we do or don't do might actually *matter* is virtually unfathomable. There is little sense that *we* need to respond.

But will we wake up one morning shocked that no one did anything, and sickened that *we* didn't?

Daniel J. Boorstin once noted that millions of Americans sit placidly before their

CNN Breaking News

TV when they might be participants. They feel a sense of helplessness. "We are tempted to become spectators. . . . We see so much, every day on the screen, of catastrophes that we can do nothing about—floods, fires, terrorist attacks, kidnappings, starvation and corruption—that we make these the very prototypes of experience. A world to be looked at, to be entertained by (or alarmed or shocked by). But not a world to act in."[5]

But it *is* a world to act in, and when you act as salt and light, it *matters.*

Let's go back to New York. In the 1980s, New York City was in the grip of one of the worst crime epidemics in its history. But then, suddenly and without warning, from a high in 1990, the crime rate went into a dramatic decline. Murders dropped by two-thirds. Felonies were cut in half. Why? The most intriguing candidate is called the "Broken Windows" theory, the brainchild of criminologists James Q. Wilson and George Kelling. They argued that crime is the inevitable result of disorder. If a window is broken and left unrepaired, people walking by will conclude that that no one cares and no one is in charge. Soon, more windows will be broken, and a sense of anarchy will spread from the building to the street it faces, sending a signal that anything goes. The idea is that crime is contagious. It can start with a broken window and spread to an entire community. This means that what matters are the *little* things; what becomes critical are *small* stands against the spread of crime—which is exactly how New York City addressed the problem. The war was waged on broken windows and graffiti, focusing on the subways. The cleanup took from 1984 to 1990. It soon spread to the entire city. Seemingly inconsequential enforcements of relatively minor infractions, such as turnstile-jumping on the subways, the "squeegee men" at intersections, public drunkenness and littering, were targeted. To the surprise of all, crime began to fall in the city.[6]

When we live like salt and light, with lives infused by Christ, it affects the world around us in disproportionate measure. We become the mended windows and the scrubbed-off graffiti. The key to making a difference is not a massive program but what some have called the "monastic option"—humble, deliberate acts of cultural preservation.[7] This is precisely what a deepened soul with a developed mind, following God's call and rooted in a church, accomplishes. Small, individual acts of living like and for Christ.

Henri Nouwen writes of a church building site where monks were working closely together with some good-natured but cursing workers. He wondered how the monks would react. He knew how *he* would react. He would not say anything at first but slowly get angry until he finally exploded: "Don't you know you are not supposed to curse!" Then everyone would be angry, the air would be tense and charity would be nonexistent. While Nouwen contemplated such things, a monk by the name of Anthony *did* respond. After having heard the name of Jesus used "in vain" several times from one particular man, Anthony walked quietly to the man, put his arm around his shoulder and said, "Hey, you know—this is a monastery—and we love that man here." The man looked up at him, smiled and said, "To tell you the truth—I do too." And they both had a good laugh.[8]

And from that simple exchange, everything changed.

THE CULTURE WE DESERVE

Jacques Barzun provocatively titled a collection of essays *The Culture We Deserve.*[9] His contention was that culture is a reflection of who we are—choices we've made, attitudes we've taken, priorities we've established. Whatever culture we have, we deserve. He was right.

Jonathan Rauch, in an article for the *Atlantic Monthly*, coined a term to describe his own spiritual condition. After a couple of glasses of Merlot, someone asked him about his religion. He was about to say "atheist" when it dawned on him that this wasn't quite accurate. "I used to call myself an atheist," he ended up responding, "and I still don't believe in God, but the larger truth is that it has been years since I really cared one way or another. I'm"—and this was when it hit him—"an . . . apatheist!" Rauch went on to describe his state as a "disinclination to care all that much about one's own religion, and an even stronger disinclination to care about other people's." He notes that it is more of an attitude than a belief system. He has the culture he deserves.

And the Christian? Consider Rauch's next words. "I have Christian friends who organize their lives around an intense and personal relationship with God, but who betray no sign of caring that I am an unrepentantly atheistic Jewish homosexual. They are exponents, at least, of the second, more important part of apatheism: the part that doesn't mind what other people think about God."[10]

We have the culture we deserve as well.

This is the great danger of our day. Many don't care about their souls, they don't care about their minds, they don't care about their call, they don't care about the church, which results in the most alarming state of all—not caring about a lost and decaying world. Yet caring is at the heart of what it means to live a serious life during serious times. Václav Havel, the last president of Czechoslovakia and the first president of the Czech Republic, and one of Europe's foremost playwrights and essayists, wrote to his wife: "It is not the authors of absurd plays or pessimistic poems, nor the suicides, nor people constantly afflicted by anger, boredom, anxiety, and despair, nor the alcoholics and drug addicts, who have, in the deepest sense, lost their grip on the meaning of life and become 'nonbelievers': it is people who are apathetic."[11]

But there is another way to live. As Canadian singer-songwriter Bruce Cockburn offered in the song "Lovers in a Dangerous Time," we must "kick at the darkness 'til it bleeds daylight."[12] This is why I have not wanted to offer little more than cultural lament. As Craig Gay writes, "Descriptive analysis cannot, in and of itself, generate enough spiritual energy to really challenge the modern *status quo*."[13] The purpose of understanding the serious nature of our time is to undertake a serious life, a life that not only understands the times but is then moved to act within those times for Christ. This will demand a heart that is open to this world, but also one breaking over it.

In July of 1854 the notorious Sheffield criminal Charlie Peace was taken from Armley Jail in Leeds, England, to be hung. As was custom, a ceremony on his behalf was performed by an Anglican priest just before his execution. A priest would walk behind the man condemned to death, reading aloud from the Prayer Book. Such matters had become routine, performed ritually and often without feeling. These were the words that were read: "Those who die without Christ experience hell, which is the pain of forever dying without the release which death itself can bring."

Such words, falling upon the ears of a condemned man on his way to death and offered with such a startling lack of emotion, caused Peace to stop, turn around to the priest, and ask, "What are you reading?"

"*The Consolation of Religion*," replied the priest.

"Do you believe that?"

The priest was taken aback, but after collecting himself, said, "Well . . . I . . . suppose I do."

Then Peace is recorded to have said, "Sir, if I believed what you and the church . . . say you believe about heaven and hell—even if England were covered with broken glass from coast to coast, I would walk over it, if need be on my hands and knees, and think it a worthwhile living just to save one soul from an eternal hell like that."[14]

The urgency and needed passion was clear to a nonbeliever. Is it as clear to us? God is alive and well and has spoken his truth into the world. He has stopped at nothing, including the sacrifice of his own Son, to draw the world back to himself. He calls his followers to this grand and glorious mission because it is a cause that is more than worth dying for.

It is a cause worth *living* for.

GOING FURTHER

To serve the vision of this book in an ongoing manner, a website has been developed: <www.serioustimes.com>.

At <www.serioustimes.com>, you will find an introductory reading list on the topics discussed in this book as well as a comprehensive reading list for the development of a Christian mind. Material related to serving spiritual formation, vocation and the church is also provided. Through <www.serioustimes.com> you will also be able to gain access to small group materials and study guides for use with this book, downloadable articles, learning and personal development opportunities, tapes and CDs, as well as helpful links to other websites.

ILLUSTRATION
CREDITS

INTRODUCTION

Image: Thomas Jefferson
Credit: National Portrait Gallery, Smithsonian Institution/Art Resource, NY

CHAPTER 1

Image: God handing St. Peter's keys to the pope and a sword to the emperor
Credit: Bibliotheque Nationale, Paris, France/Bridgeman Art Library Gi-
raudon/Bridgeman Art Library

Image: David
Credit: Erich Lessing/ Art Resource, NY

Image: Immanuel Kant
Credit: Hulton Archive/Getty Images

Image: William Wilberforce
Credit: Hulton Archive/Getty ImagesChapter 2

CHAPTER 2

Image: Ellis Island
Credit: The New York Public Library/Art Resource, NY

Image: Cover, *Utne Reader*
Credit: Utne Reader

Image: Cartoon by Alfred Le Petit
Credit: The New York Public Library

Image: Dietrich Bonhoeffer
Credit: Heike Kaiser Verlag

CHAPTER 3

Image: Cast of original *Star Trek*
Credit: AP/Worldwide Photos

Image: Wittgenstein's Rabbit/Duck
Credit: Maureen Tobey/InterVarsity Press

Image: Friedrich Nietzche
Credit: Hulton Archive/Getty Images

Image: Times Square
Credit: Elaina Whittenhall/InterVarsity Press

Image: Trova's *Wheel Man*
Credit: The Solomon R. Guggenheim Museum, New York

Image: St. Patrick of Ireland
Credit: Hulton Archive/Getty Images

CHAPTER 4

Image: Teresa of Ávila
Credit: Roberta Polfus

Image: Celtic cross
Credit: Cindy Bunch/InterVarsity Press

Image: St. Benedict writing his *Rule*
Credit: Ink drawing from a codex, 1138-47. MS 2'415, fo. 87r./Wurttember-
gische Landesbibliothek, Stuttgart

Image: St. Benedict

Credit: Scala/Art Resource, NY

CHAPTER 5

Image: Personification of the *quadrivium*
Credit: From a ninth-century Boethius's *Arithmetic*, Bamberg, MS Class. 5
(HJ.IV.12), fol. 9v.

Image: Bodleian Library/Oxford
Credit: Hulton Archive/Getty Images

Image: Rodin's *The Thinker*
Credit: Vanni/Art Resource, NY

Image: C. S. Lewis
Credit: InterVarsity Press

CHAPTER 6

Image: Medieval monk
Credit: Oxford, Bodleian Library, MS Bodley 602, fol. 36r (13th c)

Image: Caravaggios's *Calling of St. Matthew*
Credit: Alinari/Art Resource, NY

Image: William Borden of Yale
Credit: Archives of Billy Graham Center, Wheaton, Illinois

Image: The Brontës
Credit: Hulton Archive/Getty Images

Image: Mother Teresa
Credit: Hulton Archive/Getty Images

CHAPTER 7

Image: St. Paul's during the Blitz
Credit: Hulton Archive/Getty Images

Image: Camp meeting
Credit: Courtesy Cane Ridge Preservation Project

Image: Contemporary worship
Credit: Courtesy 2100 Productions

Image: Juvenile under arrest
Credit: Thinkstock/Getty Images

Image: Martin Luther
Credit: Roberta Polfus

CONCLUSION

Image: Kitty Genovese
Credit: AP/Worldwide Photos

Image: CNN Breaking News-9/11
Credit: AP/Worldwide Photos

NOTES

Introduction

[1]Lester J. Cappon, ed., *The Adams-Jefferson Letters* (Chapel Hill: University of North Carolina Press, 1959), p. 349, cited by David McCullough, *John Adams* (New York: Simon & Schuster, 2001), p. 285.

[2]Paul Helm, *The Callings* (Carlisle, Penn.: Banner of Truth, 1987), pp. 54-55.

[3]*The Political Writings of Thomas Paine* (New York, 1830), 1:75-82, published in *The Annals of America*, vol. 2, 1755-1783: *Resistance and Revolution* (Chicago: Encyclopaedia Britannica, 1976), p. 456.

[4]Christopher Dawson, "The Six Ages of the Church," *Christianity and European Culture*, ed. Gerald J. Russello (Washington: Catholic University of America Press, 1998), pp. 34-45.

[5]I am indebted to Vincent Strudwick, "God in Oxford," in *Theology and Spirituality*, ed. John Morgan and Jane Shaw (Richmond, Ind.: GTF Books, 2003), pp. 1-4.

Chapter One: The Second Fall

[1]While Petrarch is credited for inventing the concept of the Middle Ages, he did not use the term himself. The Latin term *medium aevum* (the "Middle Age") first appeared in the fifteenth century.

[2]Christopher Dawson, *Religion and the Rise of Western Culture* (New York: Sheed & Ward, 1950), pp. 271-72.

[3]Johan Huizinga, *The Autumn of the Middle Ages*, translated by Rodney J. Payton and Ulrich Mammitzsch (Chicago: University of Chicago Press, 1996), p. 174.

[4]On this, see Michael Wood, Bruce Cole and Adelheid Gealt, *Art of the Western World: From Ancient Greece to Post-Modernism* (New York: Touchstone, 1989), p. 38.

[5]Martin E. Marty, *A Short History of Christianity*, 2nd ed. (Philadelphia: Fortress, 1987), p. 75.

[6]See Mark A. Noll, *Turning Points: Decisive Moments in the History of Christianity* (Grand Rapids: Baker, 1997), p. 121.

[7]J. M. Roberts, The Illustrated History of the World, vol. 5, The Far East and a New Europe (New York: Oxford University Press, 1999), p. 118.

[8]See Noll, Turning Points, p. 122.

[9]See William Manchester, A World Lit Only by Fire: The Medieval Mind and the Renaissance (Boston: Little, Brown and Company, 1992), pp. 104-5.

[10]Wood, Cole and Gealt, Art of the Western World, p. 143.

[11]Fernand Braudel, A History of Civilizations, trans. Richard Mayne (New York: Penguin, 1994), p. 341.

[12]See Wood, Cole and Gealt, Art of the Western World, p. xv.

[13]William J. Bouwsma, The Waning of the Renaissance, 1550-1640, The Yale Intellectual History of the West (New Haven, Conn.: Yale University Press, 2000), pp. 112-28.

[14]Owen Chadwick, The Secularization of the European Mind in the 19th Century (Cambridge: Cambridge University Press, 1975), p. 5.

[15]Noll, Turning Points, p. 251.

[16]Peter Gay, The Enlightenment: The Rise of Modern Paganism (New York: Norton, 1966).

[17]Henry F. May, The Enlightenment in America (New York: Oxford University Press, 1976), p. xiv.

[18]See Immanuel Kant, Foundations of the Metaphysics of Morals and What Is Enlightenment, trans. Lewis White Beck (Indianapolis: Bobbs-Merrill, 1959), p. 85.

[19]It might be argued that Kant was not a philosophical empiricist, but a philosophical rationalist. In truth, he attempted to bring the two together. But we speak here more in terms of theological categories than philosophical ones. Philosophical rationalism believes that reason is the best, and often only, path to truth. In this regard, rationalism is often contrasted with empiricism, for within philosophical categories reason is often considered distinct from the senses. In theology, however, rationalism is more the conviction that revelation stands beneath human reason, if it exists at all, with reason being all-inclusive in terms of both rational thought and the senses. So theologically, one can be a rationalist and an empiricist.

[20]See Alister E. McGrath, "Enlightenment," in The Blackwell Encyclopedia

of Modern Christian Thought, ed. Alister E. McGrath (Oxford: Blackwell, 1993), pp. 150-56.

[21]May, *The Enlightenment in America*, p. xiii.

[22]One of the most balanced and informed discussions of what actually happened with Galileo comes from David C. Lindberg, "Galileo, the Church, and the Cosmos," in *When Science and Christianity Meet*, ed. David C. Lindberg and Ronald L. Numbers (Chicago: University of Chicago Press, 2003), pp. 33-60.

[23]Neil B. MacDonald, "Enlightenment," in *The Dictionary of Historical Theology*, ed. Trevor A. Hart (Grand Rapids: Eerdmans, 2000), p. 176.

[24]Alexis de Tocqueville, *The Old Regime and the French Revolution*, trans. Stuart Gilbert (Garden City, N.Y.: Doubleday, 1955), p. 149. This text was originally written in 1856.

[25]Cited by Emmet Kennedy, *A Cultural History of the French Revolution* (New Haven, Conn.: Yale University Press, 1989), p. 343. The hymn was composed by Chenier, with music by Gossec.

[26]These closing words are indebted to Gay, *Enlightenment*, p. 419.

A Hero for Humanity: The Life of William Wilberforce

[1]Kevin Belmonte, *Hero for Humanity* (Colorado Springs: NavPress, 2002), p. 73. Acknowledgment is here given to Belmonte's work for providing direction to primary and secondary sources for Wilberforce's words.

[2]Robert Isaac and Samuel Wilberforce, *The Life of William Wilberforce* (London: John Murray, 1838), 1:148-49.

[3]William Wilberforce, *The Speech of William Wilberforce, Esq., Representative for the County of York, on the Question of the Abolition of the Slave Trade* (London: Logographic Press, 1789), p. 18.

Chapter Two: The World That Lives in Us

[1]Peter Berger, *The Sacred Canopy* (Garden City, N.Y.: Doubleday, 1969).

[2]Richard John Neuhaus, *The Naked Public Square* (Grand Rapids: Eerdmans, 1984).

[3]See Martin E. Marty, *A Short History of Christianity*, 2nd ed. (Philadelphia: Fortress, 1987), pp. 222-23.

4Huston Smith, *Why Religion Matters: The Fate of the Human Spirit in an Age of Disbelief* (New York: HarperSanFrancisco, 2001), pp. 193-194.

5For an introduction to the debate, see William H. Swatos Jr. and Daniel V. A. Olson, eds., *The Secularization Debate* (Lanham, Md.: Rowman & Littlefield, 2000).

6Peter L. Berger, ed., *The Desecularization of the World* (Grand Rapids: Eerdmans, 1999), p. 2.

7Ibid., p. 10.

8Peter Berger, quoted in Huston Smith, *Why Religion Matters* (New York: HarperSanFrancisco, 2001), p. 103.

9A Harris Interactive survey of 2,306 adults as reported by Netscape News/ CNN (November 5, 2003) <http://www.harrisinteractive.com/news/all-newsbydate.asp?NewsID=693>.

10As reported by George Barna, "Morality Continues to Decay," November 3, 2003, <www.barna.org/cgi-bin/PagePressRelease.asp? Press ReleaseID =152&Reference=A>.

11Owen Chadwick, *The Secularization of the European Mind in the 19th Century* (Cambridge: Cambridge University Press, 1975), p. 9.

12Ray Kroc, quoted in *Context* 15 (1981): 6.

13Os Guinness, *The Gravedigger File: Papers on the Subversion of the Modern Church* (Downers Grove: InterVarsity Press, 1983), p. 74; cf. Thomas Luckmann, *The Invisible Religion* (New York: Macmillan, 1967). Perhaps the best investigation into this dynamic of modernity was offered by Robert Bellah et al., in *Habits of the Heart: Individualism and Commitment in American Life* (San Francisco: Harper and Row, 1985). A chronicle of America's privatization of faith can be found in Phillip L. Berman's *The Search for Meaning: Americans Talk About What They Believe and Why* (New York: Ballantine, 1990).

14See John Naisbitt and Patricia Aburdene, "Spirituality, Yes. Organized Religion, No," *Megatrends 2000* (New York: William Morrow, 1990), p. 275.

15Theodore Roszak, *Where the Wasteland Ends* (Garden City, N.Y.: Anchor, 1973), p. 412.

16Page Smith, *Killing the Spirit* (New York: Viking, 1990), p. 5.

17Bellah et al., *Habits of the Heart*, p. 221.

[18]Robert Wuthnow, *After Heaven: Spirituality in America Since the 1950s* (Berkeley: University of California Press, 1998).

[19]Berger, *Sacred Canopy*, p. 127.

[20]Guinness, *Gravedigger File*, p. 94.

[21]See Samuel Eliot Morison, Henry Steele Commager and William E. Leuchtenburg, *The Growth of the American Republic*, 7th ed. (New York: Oxford University Press, 1980), 2:108 n.3, cited by Louis Menand, *The Metaphysical Club* (New York: Farrar, Straus & Giroux, 2001), p. 381.

[22]For one of the most thorough and insightful treatments of issues related to this, see Harold Netland, *Encountering Religious Pluralism* (Downers Grove, Ill.: InterVarsity Press, 2001).

[23]Langdon Gilkey, *Through the Tempest* (Minneapolis: Fortress, 1991), p. 21.

[24]Rabbi Marc Gellman and Monsignor Thomas Hartman, *How Do You Spell God?* (New York: Morrow Junior, 1995), pp. 19-24.

[25]See Harold A. Netland, *Dissonant Voices* (Grand Rapids: Eerdmans, 1991), p. 30.

[26]Gary Stephenson, Brandon Bevil and Web staff, "Cleaning Up the Outer Banks After Hurricane Isabel," posted October 22, 2003, at <http://rdu.news14.com/shared/print/default.asp?ArID=37684>.

[27]These four marks were first suggested to my thinking by Langdon Gilkey, *Naming the Whirlwind* (Indianapolis: Bobbs-Merril, 1969), and again in a variant form by Thomas C. Oden, *After Modernity . . . What?* (Grand Rapids: Zondervan, 1990). I have used Oden's terms over Gilkey's, which speak of the geist of the modern secular world in terms of contingency, relativism, temporality and autonomy.

[28]America Online homepage, March 19, 2003, <www.aol.com>.

[29]Allan Bloom, *The Closing of the American Mind* (New York: Simon & Schuster, 1987), p. 25.

[30]See James Patterson and Peter Kim, *The Day America Told the Truth* (New York: Prentice-Hall, 1991).

[31]Dorothy L. Sayers, "The Other Six Deadly Sins," in *The Whimsical Christian* (New York: Collier, 1987), p. 157.

[32]Jean Paul Sartre, *Existentialism and Human Emotions* (New York: Citadel Press, 1957), p. 63.

33Jacques Barzun, *From Dawn to Decadence* (New York: HarperCollins, 2000), p. xv.

34Oden, *After Modernity*, p. 74, see also p. 157.

35Steve Bruce, *Religion in the Modern World* (Oxford: Oxford University Press, 1996), p. 5.

36Neil Postman, *Technopoly* (New York: Alfred A. Knopf, 1992).

37On the meaning of the words *technē* and *technitēs* see J. I. Packer, "Carpenter, Builder, Workman, Craftsman, Trade," in *The New International Dictionary of New Testament Theology*, ed. Colin Brown (Grand Rapids: Zondervan, 1986), 1:279.

38Robert Edwards, quoted by Anjana Ahuja, "God Is Not in Charge, We Are," *T2-The Times*, July 24, 2003, p. 6.

39Christopher Lasch, *The Culture of Narcissism* (New York: W. W. Norton, 1991), p. 7.

40Stanley J. Grenz, *A Primer on Postmodernism* (Grand Rapids: Eerdmans, 1996), p. 62.

41Michael Burleigh, *The Third Reich* (New York: Farrar, Straus & Giroux, 2000), p. 1.

42H. R. Rookmaaker, *Modern Art and the Death of a Culture* (Wheaton: Crossway, 1994), p. 61.

43Gerard Piel, *The Age of Science* (New York: Basic Books, 2001).

44Ian Barbour, *When Science Meets Religion* (London: SPCK, 2000), p. xi.

45Carl Sagan, *The Demon-Haunted World* (New York: Random House, 1995).

46See David C. Lindberg, *The Beginnings of Western Science* (Chicago: University of Chicago Press, 1992). This case is made throughout Lindberg's study, but note particularly the discussion on pp. 149-51.

47Colin Brown, *Christianity and Western Thought* (Downers Grove, Ill.: InterVarsity Press, 1990), 1:156.

48For example, note the popularity—and titles—of the works of Paul Davies, including *God and the New Physics* (New York: Simon & Schuster, 1983); *The Mind of God* (New York: Touchstone, 1992); and *The Fifth Miracle* (New York: Simon & Schuster, 2000).

49Voltaire, cited by Chadwick, *Secularization of the European Mind*, p. 10.

⁵⁰Christopher Dawson, *Dynamics of World History*, ed. John J. Mulloy (Wilmington, Del.: ISI Books, 2002), p. xxxi, citing *Enquiries* (London, 1933), p. vi.

⁵¹Friedrich Nietzsche's famed "God is dead" passage can be found in section 125 of *The Gay Science*, available in *The Portable Nietzsche*, ed. Walter Kaufmann (New York: Penguin, 1982), pp. 95-96.

Standing in the Storm: The Life of Dietrich Bonhoeffer

¹Dietrich Bonhoeffer, *The Cost of Discipleship*, rev. ed. (New York: Collier, 1963), p. 99.

²Noted by Os Guinness, *Prophetic Untimeliness* (Grand Rapids: Baker, 2003), p. 99.

³Cited by Franklin Sherman in "Bonhoeffer, Dietrich," *Encyclopaedia Britannica*. 2003. Encyclopaedia Britannica Premium Service, October 25, 2003 <www.britannica.com/eb/article?eu=82755>.

⁴John W. Doberstein, introduction to Bonhoeffer's *Life Together*, p. 13.

Chapter Three: The City of Dreadful Delight

¹See Judith R. Walkowitz, *The City of Dreadful Delight* (Chicago: University of Chicago Press, 1992).

²Stanley J. Grenz, *A Primer on Postmodernism* (Grand Rapids: Eerdmans, 1996), p. 9.

³See David Lyon, *Postmodernity*, 2nd ed. (Minneapolis: University of Minnesota Press, 1999), p. 9.

⁴On Barzun's reflections, see *From Dawn to Decadence* (New York: HarperCollins, 2000), particularly pp. xvi-xvii.

⁵David Harvey, *The Condition of Postmodernity* (Oxford: Blackwell, 1990), p. 116; Neil Smith cited by Harvey on p. 325.

⁶There are many treatments of the philosophy behind postmodernism. One of the more thorough is Millard J. Erickson, *Truth or Consequences* (Downers Grove, Ill.: InterVarsity Press, 2001). The best general introduction, however, remains Grenz's *A Primer on Postmodernism*.

⁷Gary Woller, ed., *Public Administration and Postmodernism*, a special issue of *American Behavioral Scientist* 41, no. 1 (1997): 9.

[8]Walter Truett Anderson, *Reality Isn't What It Used to Be* (San Francisco: Harper & Row, 1990), p. 75.

[9]See Lyon, *Postmodernity*, p. 11.

[10]See Friedrich Nietzsche, *The Will to Power*, ed. Walter Kaufmann (New York: Random House, 1967), p. 267, sec. 487.

[11]Todd Gitlin, *Media Unlimited: How the Torrent of Images and Sounds Overwhelms Our Lives* (New York: Metropolitan Books, 2001).

[12]Marshall McLuhan with Quentin Fiore, *The Medium Is the Massage* (Corte Madera, Calif.: Gingko Press, 2001), p. 26.

[13]Fred Fedler, *An Introduction to the Mass Media* (New York: Harcourt Brace Jovanovich, 1978), p. 7.

[14]Kathleen Parker, "Wonder Why Kids Have No Values? Hint: Watch TV," *Charlotte Observer*. On ways that the media are biased, see Bernard Goldberg, *Bias: A CBS Insider Exposes How the Media Distort the News* (Washington: Regnery, 2002); and Mark C. Carnes, *Past Imperfect: History According to the Movies* (New York: Henry Holt, 1995).

[15]"Oliver Stone: Forget Facts; Films Aren't About Accuracy," *Charlotte Observer*, September 23, 1997, p. 2A.

[16]Gitlin, *Media Unlimited*, pp. 6, 94.

[17]Richard Rorty, *Philosophy and the Mirror of Nature* (Princeton, N.J.: Princeton University Press, 1979), p. 393.

[18]Jean-François Lyotard, *The Postmodern Condition* (Minneapolis: University of Minnesota Press, 1984), p. xxiv.

[19]Stanley J. Grenz and John R. Franke, *Beyond Foundationalism: Shaping Theology in a Postmodern Context* (Louisville: Westminster John Knox, 2001), p. 23.

[20]Morris Berman, *The Twilight of American Culture* (New York: W. W. Norton, 2000), pp. 104-6. See Pitirim Sorokin, *Social and Cultural Dynamics* (New Brunswick: Transaction Publishers, 1991).

[21]Mitch Albom, *Tuesdays with Morrie* (New York: Doubleday, 1997), pp. 33, 84.

[22]Douglas Coupland, *Life After God* (New York: Simon & Schuster, 1994), p. 359.

[23]Christopher Dawson, *Dynamics of World History*, ed. John J. Mulloy (Wilmington, Del.: ISI Books, 2002), p. xix.

[24]James A. Herrick, *The Making of the New Spirituality* (Downers Grove, Ill.: InterVarsity Press, 2003).

[25]See Richard Shweder, "Santa Claus on the Cross," in *The Truth About the Truth*, ed. Walter Truett Anderson (New York: Putnam, 1995), p. 73.

[26]Lewis Carroll, *Alice's Adventures in Wonderland* (London: Alfred A. Knopf, 1984), p. 60.

[27]Connie Zweig, "The Death of the Self in a Postmodern World," in *The Truth About the Truth*, ed. Walter Truett Anderson (New York: Putnam, 1995), p. 146.

[28]C. S. Lewis, *The Abolition of Man* (New York: Collier, 1947), p. 77.

[29]Frederick Buechner, *The Magnificent Defeat* (New York: Seabury, 1979), p. 65.

[30]On this idea and use of Buechner's story, see Philip Yancey, *Disappointment with God* (Grand Rapids: Zondervan, 1988), pp. 252-53.

Come and Walk Among Us: The Life of St. Patrick

[1]*The Confession of Saint Patrick*, trans. John Skinner (New York: Doubleday, 1998), p. 45.

[2]Thomas Cahill, *How the Irish Saved Civilization* (New York: Doubleday, 1995), p. 131.

[3]Ibid., pp. 103, 108.

[4]Maire B. De Paor, *Patrick: The Pilgrim Apostle of Ireland* (New York: HarperCollins, 1998), p. 36.

Interlude

[1]Søren Kierkegaard, "The Happy Conflagration," adapted from "A" in *Either/Or*, 1:30, in *Parables of Kierkegaard*, ed. Thomas C. Oden (Princeton, NJ: Princeton University Press, 1978), p. 3.

[2]The Greek language actually has a number of terms which express the experience of time, with the most extensive being *aion*, which refers to an extended period of time. *Chronos* refers to the quantitative, linear understanding of time. It is this formal, scientific understanding of time that is the most compatible with our modern use of the word. *Kairos*, however, refers to the content of time. For more on the background of this word, see Walter Bauer,

"καιρός," in *A Greek-English Lexicon of the New Testament and Other Early Christian Literature*, ed. and trans. William F. Arndt and F. Wilbur Gingrich (Chicago: University of Chicago Press, 1958), pp. 394-95; Gerhard Delling, "Καιρός," in *Theological Dictionary of the New Testament*, ed. Gerhard Kittel, trans. Geoffrey W. Bromiley (Grand Rapids: Eerdmans, 1965), 3:455-62; Colin Brown, ed., *The New International Dictionary of New Testament Theology* (Grand Rapids: Zondervan, 1988), 3:833-39.
[3]For more on the application of this idea, see the author's *Life-Defining Moments* (Colorado Springs: WaterBrook, 2001).
[4]Os Guinness, *The American Hour* (New York: Free Press, 1993), p. 396.
[5]H. Richard Niebuhr, *Christ & Culture* (New York: Harper & Row, 1951).
[6]Thomas Kelly, *A Testament of Devotion* (New York: Harper & Row, 1941), p. 47.
[7]Ralph C. Wood, *Contending for the Faith* (Waco, Tex.: Baylor University Press, 2003), pp. 26-27.
[8]Peter Kreeft, *How to Win the Culture War* (Downers Grove, Ill.: InterVarsity Press, 2002), p. 102.
[9]*New Wineskins* <www.wineskins.org/content.asp?CID=28179>.

Chapter Four: Deepening Our Souls

[1]Thomas Merton, *Thoughts in Solitude* (New York: Farrar, Straus & Giroux, 1958), p. 46.
[2]Marjorie J. Thompson, *Soul Feast: An Invitation to the Christian Spiritual Life* (Louisville, Ky.: Westminster John Knox Press, 1995), p. 6.
[3]Frederick Buechner, *A Room Called Remember* (San Francisco: Harper & Row, 1984), p. 38.
[4]Robert Louis Wilken, *The Spirit of Early Christian Thought* (New Haven: Yale University Press, 2003), p. xxii.
[5]Douglas V. Steere, *Prayer and Worship* (Richmond, Ind.: Friends United Press, 1978), p. 2.
[6]Dallas Willard, *The Spirit of the Disciplines* (New York: HarperSanFrancisco, 1988), pp. ix, 3-5.
[7]Francis de Sales, *Introduction to the Devout Life*, trans. John K. Ryan (New York: Doubleday, 1989) p. 37.

8Richard J. Foster, *The Celebration of Discipline* (San Francisco: Harper & Row, 1978), p. 1.

9Thomas Kelly, *A Testament of Devotion* (New York: Harper & Row, 1941).

10Henri J. M. Nouwen, *The Genesee Diary* (New York: Doubleday, 1981), p. 107.

11Simon Chan, *Spiritual Theology* (Downers Grove, Ill.: InterVarsity Press, 1998), p. 159.

12Ken Gire, *The Reflective Life* (Colorado Springs: Chariot Victor, 1998), p. 89.

13Thompson, *Soul Feast*, p. 18.

14*The Rule of St. Benedict*, ed. Timothy Fry (New York: Vintage, 1998), p. 3.

15Luke Dysinger, "Accepting the Embrace of God: The Ancient Art of *Lectio Divina*," St. Andrew's Abbey homepage <www.valyermo.com/ld-art.html>.

16Karl Barth, *Prayer* (Philadelphia: Westminster Press, 1952), p. 23. Perry LeFevre, *Understandings of Prayer* (Philadelphia: Westminster Press, 1981), p. 35. Thomas Merton, *Contemplative Prayer* (Garden City, N.Y.: Doubleday, 1971), p. 67. Geoffrey Wainwright, "Types of Spirituality," in *The Study of Spirituality*, ed. Cheslyn Jones, Geoffrey Wainwright and Edward Yarnold (New York: Oxford University Press, 1986), p. 592.

17Francis de Sales, *Treatise on the Love of God*, trans. Henry Benedict Mackey (Rockford, Ill.: Tan Books, 1997), p. 231.

18Douglas V. Steere, *On Being Present Where You Are*, Pendle Hill Pamphlet 151 (Wallingford, Penn.: Pendle Hill, 1967), p. 17.

19Teresa of Ávila, *A Life of Prayer*, ed. by James Houston (Portland, Ore.: Multnomah Press, 1983), p. 2, cited by Chan, *Spiritual Theology*, p. 137.

20Thomas Merton, *The Wisdom of the Desert* (London: Sheldon Press, 1961), 13:30.

21Frederick Buechner, *Whistling in the Dark* (San Francisco: Harper & Row, 1988), pp. 97-98.

22Esther de Waal, *Every Earthly Blessing* (Harrisburg, Penn.: Morehouse, 1999), p. 37.

23On Celtic beliefs see Timothy Joyce, *Celtic Christianity* (Marynoll, N.Y.: Orbis, 1998).

24De Sales, *Introduction to the Devout Life*, pp. 89-90.

25E. Glenn Hinson, "At Eternity's Converging Point," *Weavings* 17, no. 3 (2002): 27.

[26]De Sales, *Introduction to the Devout Life*, p. 45.

[27]Jeannette A. Bakke, *Holy Invitations* (Grand Rapids: Baker, 2000), pp. 31-33.

[28]Joyce, *Celtic Christianity*, p. 45. For an excellent and highly accessible overview of the history of spiritual direction, see Chris Armstrong and Steven Gertz, "Christian History Corner: Got Your 'Spiritual Director' Yet?" *Christianity Today* online, May 2, 2003 <www.christianityto-day.com/ct/2003/117/51.0/html>.

[29]Eugene Peterson, *Working the Angles* (Grand Rapids: Eerdmans, 1987), p. 103.

[30]See Thompson, *Soul Feast*, pp. 104-5.

[31]Mark A. Noll, *Turning Points* (Grand Rapids: Baker, 1997), p. 84.

[32]Thomas Moore, in *The Rule of St. Benedict*, ed. Timothy Fry (New York: Random House, 1998), p. xvi.

[33]Foster, *Celebration of Discipline*, p. 6.

Seeking God: The Life of St. Benedict

[1]See *The Rule of St. Benedict*, ed. Timothy Fry (New York: Random House, 1998), p. xvi.

[2]Thomas Moore, in *The Rule of St. Benedict*, p. xxviii.

[3]Mark A. Noll, *Turning Points* (Grand Rapids: Baker, 1997), p. 84.

Chapter Five: Developing Our Minds

[1]These statistics are adapted from Morris Berman, *The Twilight of American Culture* (New York: W. W. Norton, 2000), pp. 33-36.

[2]Harry Blamires, *The Christian Mind* (Ann Arbor, Mich.: Servant, 1978), p. 3.

[3] Mark A. Noll, *The Scandal of the Evangelical Mind* (Grand Rapids: Eerdmans, 1994), p. 3.

[4]See Richard Hofstadter, *Anti-Intellectualism in American Life* (New York: Vintage, 1962), pp. 55-80.

[5]John R. W. Stott, *Your Mind Matters* (Downers Grove, Ill.: InterVarsity Press, 1972), p. 13.

[6]On this, see Ray C. Petry, ed., *Late Medieval Mysticism*, Library of Christian Classics, Ichthus Edition (Philadelphia: Westminster Press, 1957), pp. 44-45.

[7]Jean Leclercq, *The Love of Learning and the Desire for God*, trans. Catharine Misrahi (New York: Fordham University Press, 1982), p. 22.

[8]On this see Ralph M. McInerny, *A Student's Guide to Philosophy* (Wilmington, Del.: ISI Books, 1999), pp. 18-19.

[9]Noll, *Scandal of the Evangelical Mind*, p. 34.

[10]Thomas Morris, interviewed by Stephen N. Williams, "Public Intellectual: An Interview with Tom Morris," *Books & Culture* 9, no. 1 (2003): 35.

[11]For example, see Stephen Jay Gould, *I Have Landed* (New York: Harmony Books, 2002), p. 214.

[12]Stephen Jay Gould, *I Have Landed: The End of a Beginning in Natural History* (New York: Harmony, 2002), p. 214.

[13]Brian L. Silver, *The Ascent of Science* (Oxford: Oxford University Press, 1998), p. xiv.

[14]Noll, *Scandal of the Evangelical Mind*, p. 7.

[15]Jonathan Edwards, "Notes on the Mind," in *The Works of Jonathan Edwards: Scientific and Philosophical Writings*, ed. Wallace E. Anderson (New Haven, Conn.: Yale University Press, 1980), pp. 341-42. The best biography to date on Edwards is by George M. Marsden, *Jonathan Edwards* (New Haven, Conn.: Yale, University Press 2003).

[16]Thomas C. Oden, *After Modernity . . . What?* (Grand Rapids: Zondervan, 1990), p. 68.

[17]On how "worldview" has been treated by a variety of thinkers, see David K. Naugle, *Worldview: The History of a Concept* (Grand Rapids: Eerdmans, 2002).

[18]Brian J. Walsh and J. Richard Middleton, *The Transforming Vision* (Downers Grove, Ill.: InterVarsity Press, p. 35.

[19]Wittgenstein's simile is found in Anthony C. Thiselton, *The Two Horizons* (Grand Rapids: Eerdmans, 1980), p. 199.

[20]See Michael Polanyi, *The Tacit Dimension* (Gloucester, Mass.: Peter Smith, 1983); *Personal Knowledge* (Chicago: University of Chicago Press, 1974); Michael Polanyi with Harry Prosch, *Meaning* (Chicago: University of Chicago Press, 1977).

[21]Quentin J. Schultze, *Habits of the High-Tech Heart* (Grand Rapids: Baker, 2002), p. 21.

22"Some Perspective, Please," *World* 12, no. 18 (1997): 9.

23Cass Sunstein, *Republic.Com* (Princeton, NJ: Princeton University Press, 2001).

24Owen Chadwick, *The Secularization of the European Mind in the 19th Century* (Cambridge: Cambridge University Press, 1975), p. 164.

25Susan Wise Bauer, *The Well-Educated Mind* (New York: W. W. Norton, 2003), p. 15.

26Cited by Daniel J. Boorstin, *The Discoverers* (New York: Random House, 1983), p. 492.

27Robert Maynard Hutchins, *The Great Conversation: The Substance of a Liberal Education*, Great Books of the Western World, 54 vols. (Chicago: Encyclopaedia Britannica, Inc., 1952), 1:xi. The series has been updated to include such modern luminaries as Kafka, Barth, Wittgenstein, Einstein, Proust, Heidegger and Weber.

28Rene Descartes, Discourse on Method, I, *The Essential Descartes*, ed. Margaret D. Wilson (New York: Meridian/New American Library, 1969), p. 109.

29Arthur Schopenhauer, *Some Forms of Literature*, as cited by Mortimer Adler and Charles Van Doren in *Great Treasury of Western Thought* (New York: R. R. Bowker, 1977), p. 1021.

30See Hutchins, *The Great Conversation*, p. xi.

31Fred Fedler, *An Introduction to the Mass Media* (New York: Harcourt Brace Jovanovich, 1978), p. 5.

32Brandon Tartikoff, quoted by Paul C. Light, *Baby Boomers* (New York: W. W. Norton, 1988), p. 123.

33*New York Times*, August 24, 1997, cited in *The Pastor's Weekly Briefing* 5, no. 35 (1997): 2.

34See Neil Postman, *Amusing Ourselves to Death* (New York: Penguin, 1985), p. vii.

35Bauer, *Well-Educated Mind*, pp. 22-23.

36Neil Postman, *The Disappearance of Childhood* (New York: Vintage, 1994), p. 116.

37Søren Kirkegaard, cited by John Lukacs, *A Student's Guide to the Study of History*, ISI Guides to the Major Disciplines (Wilmington, Del.: ISI

Books, 2000), p. 3.

[38]Os Guinness, "Knowing Means Doing: A Challenge to Think Christianly," *Radix* 18, no. 1 (1987), as cited by James W. Sire, *Discipleship of the Mind: Learning to Love God in the Ways We Think* (Downers Grove: InterVarsity Press, 1990), p. 23.

[39]Stott, *Your Mind Matters*, p. 52.

A Most Converted Mind: The Life of C. S. Lewis

[1]See Roger Lancelyn Green and Walter Hooper, *C. S. Lewis*, rev. ed. (New York: Harvest, 1994); David C. Downing, *The Most Reluctant Convert* (Downers Grove, Ill.: InterVarsity Press, 2002); George Sayer, *Jack: C. S. Lewis and His Times* (New York: Harper & Row, 1988); and Lewis's own spiritual biography, *Surprised by Joy* (New York: Harvest, 1955).

[2]Walter Hooper, preface to C. S. Lewis, *God in the Dock*, ed. Walter Hooper (Grand Rapids: Eerdmans, 1970), p. 12.

[3]Green and Hooper, *C. S. Lewis*, p. 209.

[4]C. S. Lewis, *Mere Christianity* (New York: MacMillan, 1952), p. vii.

Chapter Six: Answering the Call

[1]Os Guinness, *The Call* (Nashville: Word, 1998), p. 4.

[2]Owen Chadwick, *The Secularization of the European Mind in the 19th Century* (Cambridge: Cambridge University Press, 1975), p. 8.

[3]Gene Edward Veith Jr., *God at Work* (Wheaton, Ill.: Crossway, 2002), p. 19.

[4]Henri J. M. Nouwen, *The Genesee Diary* (New York: Doubleday, 1981), p. 28.

[5]On this see Guinness, *Call*, p. 31.

[6]Dorothy L. Sayers, "Creed or Chaos?" in *The Whimsical Christian* (New York: Macmillan, 1978), p. 50.

[7]Parker J. Palmer, *Let Your Life Speak: Listening for the Voice of Vocation* (San Francisco: Jossey-Bass, 2000), p. 4.

[8]See Martin Buber, *Tales of the Hasidim* (New York: Schocken, 1975), p. 251.

[9]Thomas Merton, *New Seeds of Contemplation* (New York: New Direc-

tions Publishing, 1961), p. 29.

[10]William D. Romanowski, *Eyes Wide Open: Looking for God in Popular Culture* (Grand Rapids: Brazos/Baker, 2001), p. 81.

[11]Frederick Buechner, *Wishful Thinking* (New York: Harper & Row, 1973), p. 95.

[12]John Calvin, cited by Paul Helm, *The Callings* (Carlisle, Penn.: Banner of Truth, 1987), p. 103.

[13]Henri J. M. Nouwen, *The Genesee Diary* (New York: Doubleday, 1981), p p. 78.

[14]Merton, *New Seeds*, p. 47.

[15]Adapted from Mrs. Howard Taylor, *Borden of Yale '09* (London: China Inland Mission, 1927). See also the fall 1970 edition of *The Yale Standard*.

[16]Walter Brueggemann, *Hopeful Imagination*, cited by Kathleen Norris, *Cloister Walk* (New York: Riverhead, 1996), p. 41.

[17]Esther de Waal, *Seeking God* (Collegeville, Minn.: Liturgical Press, 2001), p. 43.

[18]Thomas R. Kelly, *A Testament of Devotion* (New York: Harper & Row, 1941), p. 61.

[19]Ibid., p. 72.

[20]Nouwen, *Genesee Diary*, p. 76.

[21]See Veith, *God at Work*, p. 23.

Something Beautiful for God: The Life of Mother Teresa

[1]On the life of Mother Teresa, see Malcolm Muggeridge, *Something Beautiful for God* (San Francisco: Harper & Row, 1971); and Mother Teresa, *In the Heart of the World*, ed. Becky Benenate (Novato, Calif.: New World Library, 1997).

[2]David Aikman, *Great Souls* (Dallas: Word, 1998), p. 197, and quoting Mother Teresa, p. 192.

[3]Muggeridge, *Something Beautiful for God*, p. 21.

[4]Mother Teresa of Calcutta, *My Life for the Poor* (New York: Ballantine, 1985), p. 102.

[5]Muggeridge, *Something Beautiful for God*, p. 146.

[6]Ibid., p. 104.

Chapter Seven: Aligning with the Church

[1]Peter Berger, "The Desecularization of the World: A Global Overview," in *The Desecularization of the World*, ed. Peter Berger (Grand Rapids: Eerdmans, 1999), p. 4.

[2]Dennis Hollinger, "The Church as Apologetic: A Sociology of Knowledge Perspective," in *Christian Apologetics in the Postmodern World*, ed. Timothy R. Phillips and Dennis L. Okholm (Downers Grove, Ill.: InterVarsity Press, 1995), p. 183.

[3]Lesslie Newbigin, *The Gospel in a Pluralist Society* (Grand Rapids: Eerdmans, 1989), p. 227.

[4]Wesley K. Willmer, J. David Schmidt and Martyn Smith, *The Prospering Parachurch* (San Francisco: Jossey-Bass, 1998), p. xii.

[5]Willmer, Schmidt and Smith, *Prospering Parachurch*, p. xiv.

[6]Newbigin, *Gospel in a Pluralist Society*, p. 141.

[7]Richard J. Mouw, *Consulting the Faithful: What Christian Intellectuals Can Learn from Popular Religion* (Grand Rapids: Eerdmans, 1994), p. 17.

[8]Nathan O. Hatch, *The Democratization of American Christianity* (New Haven, Conn.: Yale University Press, 1989), p. 13.

[9]Ibid., p. 50.

[10]Ibid., pp. 55, 209.

[11]On this, see James Gilbert, *Redeeming Culture: American Religion in an Age of Science* (Chicago: University of Chicago Press, 1997), p. 124.

[12]Millard Erickson, *Christian Theology* (Grand Rapids: Baker, 1985), pp. 113-16.

[13]Charles Colson with Ellen Santilli Vaughn, *The Body* (Dallas: Word, 1992), p. 48. This book was recently revised and released as *Being the Body* (Nashville: W Group, 2003).

[14]Geoffrey Wainwright, *Doxology: The Praise of God in Worship, Doctrine, and Life* (New York: Oxford University Press, 1980), pp. 2, 3.

[15]Richard J. Foster, *The Celebration of Discipline* (San Francisco: Harper & Row, 1978), p. 148.

[16]Jeffrey Burton Russell, *A History of Medieval Christianity: Prophecy and Order* (Arlington Heights, Ill.: Harlan Davidson, 1968), pp. 32-33.

[17]Lee Strobel, *Inside the Mind of Unchurched Harry and Mary* (Grand Rap-

ids: Zondervan, 1993), pp. 85-91.

[18]Michael Green, *Evangelism in the Early Church* (Grand Rapids: Eerdmans, 1970), p. 173.

[19]This story is adapted from Bill Hybels, *Courageous Leadership* (Grand Rapids: Zondervan, 2002), pp. 18-21.

[20]Ibid., p. 21.

The Wild Boar in the Vineyard: The Life of Martin Luther

[1]See the highly accessible biography of Luther by Roland H. Bainton, *Here I Stand* (New York: Abingdon, 1950).

[2]See Graham Tomlin, *Luther and His World* (Downers Grove, Ill.: InterVarsity Press, 2002), p. 71.

[3]Ibid., p. 99.

[4]Ibid., p. 117.

[5]See Richard Marius, *Martin Luther* (Cambridge, Mass.: Belknap Press, 1999), p. 383.

[6]Some have discounted this claim toward Luther, saying that people have confused "bar tunes" with "bar forms"—the first would be a tune straight from the taverns, the second simply the form of music for the day. The distinction is accurate, the conclusion, however, remains. This "bar form" would have been much more familiar to those actually in the bars, which is undoubtedly what Luther had in mind.

[7]Bainton, *Here I Stand*, pp. 301-2.

Conclusion

[1]Robert D. Kaplan, *An Empire Wilderness* (New York: Vintage, 1998), pp. 181, 182.

[2]See Alvin J. Schmidt, *Under the Influence: How Christianity Transformed Civilization* (Grand Rapids: Zondervan, 2001), as well as the foreword to the book by Paul L. Maier from which this paragraph is particularly indebted.

[3]On the many stories and commentaries surrounding the slaying of Kitty Genovese, see Michael Dorman, "The Killing of Kitty Genovese," in *Long Island: Our Story* <www.lihistory.com>.

[4]See Malcolm Gladwell, *The Tipping Point* (Boston: Little, Brown, 2000), pp. 27-28.

[5]Daniel J. Boorstin, "The Road to Diplopia," *TV Guide* 26 (1978), p. 14, cited by Dennis K. Davis and Stanley J. Baran, *Mass Communication and Everyday Life* (Belmont, Calif.: Wadsworth, 1981), p. 98.

[6]See Gladwell, *The Tipping Point*, pp. 133-68. Gladwell calls this phenomenon the "Power of Context."

[7]See Morris Berman, *Twilight of American Culture* (New York: W. W. Norton, 2000); and T. S. Eliot, *Christianity and Culture* (New York: Harcourt Brace, 1976).

[8]Henri J. M. Nouwen, *The Genesee Diary* (New York: Doubleday, 1981), pp. 178-79.

[9]Jacques Barzun, *The Culture We Deserve*, ed. Arthur Krystal (Middletown, Conn.: Wesleyan University Press, 1989).

[10]Jonathan Rauch, "Let It Be," *Atlantic Monthly*, May 2003, p. 34.

[11]Václav Havel, *Letters to Olga*, trans. Paul Wilson (London: Faber & Faber, 1990), p. 235.

[12]Bruce Cockburn, "Lovers in a Dangerous Time," from the album *Stealing Fire* (1984).

[13]Craig Gay, *The Way of the (Modern) World* (Grand Rapids: Eerdmans, 1998), p. 265.

[14]Adapted from several sources, including Leonard Ravenhill, *Why Revival Tarries* (Minneapolis: Bethany House, 1979), and Tony Campolo, *Let Me Tell You a Story* (Nashville: Word, 2000), pp. 102-3.

Index

Roe v. *Wade*, 71
Roman Catholic Church, 28
Roman Catholic, Roman Catholics, 36
Roman Empire, 19, 79
Roman, Rome, 18-20, 22-23, 36, 46, 67, 79, 94, 107
Romanowski, William, 120
Rookmaaker, H. R., 46
Rorty, Richard, 60
Rosenthal, Abe, 155
Roszak, Theodore, 37
Rousseau, Jean Jacques, 29, 107
Rule of St. Benedict; spiritual rule, 85, 90-91, 94
Russell, Bertrand, 33
Sagan, Carl, 47
saint, saints, 29, 66, 73, 76, 80, 83, 89, 95, 130-31
Samuel, 122
Sankey, Ira, 140
Sartre, Jean Paul, 43
Sayers, Dorothy L., 43, 117, 153
Schaeffer, Francis, 24, 45
Schopenhauer, Arthur, 108
Schultze, Quentin, 104
Schumacher, E. F., 35
Schwartz, Morrie, 62
science, scientists, 18, 20, 22, 27, 28, 34, 41, 45-48, 60, 101-102, 118, 134, 154
Scientific American, 46
scientism, 48
Screwtape Letters, The, 114
Scripture, 10, 13, 49, 78, 81-83, 101, 104, 111, 122-123, 135, 139, 141, 150. *See* Bible
Seay, Chris, 76
"second" fall, 17-18, 29

secular, 18, 21, 24, 28, 34
secularism, 15, 34-37, 63
secularization, process of, 34-35, 37, 134
secularization "thesis," 35
self, 21, 44, 46, 64, 77, 97, 105-7, 120, 122, 125, 134, 148
sensate, 61
Serious Call to a Devout and Holy Life, A, 79
sex, sexual, 37, 59, 65
Shakespeare, William, 75, 107
silence, 75, 80, 85-86
Silver, Brian, 101
Sisters of Loretto, 130
Situation Ethics, 42
skepticism, 26, 29, 60, 63, 138
slavery, slave trade, 15, 30, 31, 66, 154
Smith, Neil, 55
Smith, Huston, 35
Smith, Page, 38
society, 20-21, 25, 36, 39-40, 42, 94, 117, 138, 148
solitude, 80, 85-86, 94
Soprano, Tony; *Sopranos*, 75-76
Sorokin, Pitirim, 61
spiritual direction, 80, 88-90
spirituality, 19, 38, 63, 80, 83, 98
St. Paul's Cathedral, 134
Stafford, William, 115
Stalin, Stalinist era, 35
Star Trek, 54
Steere, Douglas, 79, 83
Steptoe, Patrick, 45
Stone, Oliver, 58
Stott, John R. W., 98, 112

Strobel, Lee, 145
Sunstein, Cass, 105
supernatural, supernaturalism, 66-67, 143
Sweden, 36, 143
syncretism, 40
Tartikoff, Brandon, 110
technites, techne, 44
technology, technological, 44-45, 47, 53, 64-65, 101, 105, 143
"technopoly," 44
television (TV), 38, 58, 62, 76, 92, 110, 145, 153-54, 157
Temple of Reason, 29
Ten Boom, Corrie, 12, 123
Tenant of Wildfell Hall, The, 127
Teresa, Mother, 12, 105, 123, 130, 131
Teresa of Ávila, 84
Tertullian, 99, 137
Testament of Devotion, A, 81
test-tube baby, 45
theocracy, 20, 70
Theodosius, 20
theology, 20, 27, 71, 135-36
therapy, therapeutic, 45-46
Thinker, The, 111
Thomas Aquinas, 19
Thomas, Dylan, 153
Thompson, Marjorie L., 75, 82
Time, 105, 130
Times (of London), *The*, 45
Tocqueville, Alexis de, 28
Tolkien, J. R. R., 113
Tolstoy, Leo, 75
Trinity, The, 78
trivium, 100
Trova, Ernest, 64-65
truth, 18, 19, 21, 24, 28, 39-